ITALIAN
Moms

Sunday, December 10
344/021
Here's what's cookin'
Recipe from:
QUANTITY
Lisa
FIATONE
Lisa
PASTA dentro
cup of sugar
cup of oil
cup of flour

ITALIAN *Moms*

SOMETHING
OLD,
SOMETHING
NEW

*150 Family
Recipes*

ELISA COSTANTINI

with FRANK COSTANTINI

"Sons are the anchors of a mother's life."

–SOPHOCLES

STERLING EPICURE
New York

An Imprint of Sterling Publishing Co., Inc.
1166 Avenue of the Americas
New York, NY 10036

ISBN 978-1-4549-2798-3

Distributed in Canada by Sterling Publishing Co., Inc.
c/o Canadian Manda Group, 664 Annette Street
Toronto, Ontario M6S 2C8, Canada
Distributed in the United Kingdom by GMC Distribution Services
Castle Place, 166 High Street, Lewes, East Sussex BN7 1XU, England
Distributed in Australia by NewSouth Books
45 Beach Street, Coogee NSW 2034, Australia

For information about custom editions, special sales, and premium and corporate purchases,
please contact Sterling Special Sales at 800-805-5489 or specialsales@sterlingpublishing.com.

Manufactured in China

2 4 6 8 10 9 7 5 3 1

sterlingpublishing.com

Interior design by Lorie Pagnozzi
Cover design by Jo Obarowski

Food, cover, and location photography © David and Gabriela Versano; additional photography
by Christopher Bain/© Sterling Publishing: ii, iii, ix, 3 (right), 23, 42, 67; © Brent Hofacker/
Shutterstock: 25; Historic images courtesy Elisa and Frank Costantini.

DEDICATED TO THE MEMORY
OF MY DAUGHTER

AGNES MARIE

MAY 13, 1964–MAY 30, 1981

*"Child loss is not an event;
it is an indescribable
journey of survival."*

—AUTHOR UNKNOWN

S.S. Independence 1961

Contents

Foreword

To think of this work as just a cookbook would be a tremendous mistake, because it is much more. It really is an illumination of Italian culture. As in any culture, remembering the soul-warming recipes from childhood, even when and where they were enjoyed, becomes part of our collective family history and our heritage. All play an essential role in who we eventually become. This book continues Elisa's love story of family and food—her family legacy and her extraordinary recipe for giving back to others.

As a host on QVC, I am often approached by authors and agents of Italian cookbooks, who are hoping for a review and possible airings. I grew up in an Italian home, and I'm the firstborn American citizen in my family. As in Elisa's family, we still have deep Italian roots and customs, and, of course, we enjoy traditional foods. And so, it makes sense that I am always leery of "Italian" cookbooks that might not be authentic. And then, along came Elisa's first book, *Italian Moms: Spreading Their Art to Every Table*. As I began to read it, childhood memories—of holiday and Sunday dinners, clear summer days in Italy baking all day long with my Nonna, and so much more—came flooding back. I had finally found a cookbook author and a cookbook that I could be proud to present.

As we started our show, Elisa was not overwhelmed with cameras, sets, and television hoopla: She simply wanted to cook, and cook she did! She fluttered around our studio kitchen—mixing, stirring, serving, and, all the while, sharing intimate stories of her children, her grandchildren, and her husband. How she came to this country, and stories about her charming life in Italy as a young girl, were all given to us as a gift. I was so proud of the show and amazed that Elisa was able to deliver her message of love through food. She did it effortlessly and genuinely.

After the show, in true Italian fashion, Elisa invited me and my husband to her home for family Sunday dinner. A mere two weeks later, we found ourselves knocking on her front door. The experience reminded me of what my childhood friends would say when they came to my front door—"We can smell your Ma's cooking from out here!" We both knew that behind Elisa's front door, heaven was waiting!

We were greeted by the entire family, of course. The children, nieces, nephews, grandchildren, and family friends were all there to welcome us in. There was an immediate sense of acceptance and love. No one was missing; after all, it was Sunday dinner! The aroma that whirled through the home was indescribable, but familiar. My mother's home and my Nonna's home smelled the same. Instantly, fresh basil, sweet tomatoes, robust meats, and flavorful cheeses transported me to another magical time and place. One table wasn't large enough to hold all the loving generations, so multiple tables were strung together from the kitchen into the dining room and the living room. There was a place for everyone.

The meal went on forever, with multiple mouthwatering courses that kept our plates full. The atmosphere was filled with joy. There was generosity of self and, most importantly, love. Every Sunday, members of the Costantini family share their stories, hopes, dreams, and their love for each other, and Elisa is the glue. Through her food, she holds several generations together, and they reciprocate by being present and being wholeheartedly invested.

Elisa was raised this way, a long time ago in Italy, and she knows the importance of the gathering. She is keeping tradition alive within her family, and she wants to share it with everyone. And that is just what she is doing in this new book! *Italian Moms: Something Old, Something New* gives you memories and traditions of a true Italian kitchen; it shares the history of celebrations; it encourages generations to work together; and it invites the younger generations to make traditions of their own. Most of all, it brings family and friends, new and old, together around a table of great food and love.

Enjoy!
—Antonella Nester

Introduction

Of all the things I ever imagined doing in my life, I can honestly say that writing a cookbook, let alone two, was *not* among them. If I look back over the past couple of years since *Italian Moms: Spreading Their Art to Every Table* was published, however, I quickly realize that this whole journey fits a recurring theme in my life—I tend to go into things kicking and screaming, only to come out the other side much happier and appreciative of the bounties I received along the way. What they say about hindsight—that you only appreciate what you have looking back on it from the perspective of a later time—is true. Yet, looking backward can also be dangerous. You could look back, reflect on all the work it took to get there, and wonder if you would ever do it again, given the chance. Such a stance might stop you from moving forward, even if you truly got to a much better place despite all the hard work.

My work on *Italian Moms* is a good example, and so is the story of my time here in America. As readers of my previous book know, I was a reluctant immigrant who came to appreciate life in my adopted country only much later in life. I could easily look back over the period of time from the moment I stepped off the SS *Independence*, in 1961, to today, catalog all the hard times and sorrows that life entailed, and regret that the journey ever took place. But to do so would also erase all the fond memories of time spent with cherished loved ones; it would mean vanquishing from thought both the small and large moments of joy involving my family; and most of all, it would mean ignoring the fact that, after all is said and done, and despite all the ups and downs, I have lived a terrific life.

If I look at the time spent working on my first cookbook, I can likewise reflect on all the hard work and the strangeness of a process that was contrary to my naive sensibilities. But, to do so would mean erasing the joy and fun I had collaborating with my son Frank; it would mean never giving myself the chance to recall the stories of my life that were conjured up in the process; and it would mean ignoring the blessings that the book brought into my life since it became a reality.

And those blessings have been many! After I lost my dear husband, Francesco, on Christmas Eve in 2013, I was deeply despondent. After what seemed like a lifetime of struggle, the blow of losing my cherished husband seemed just too much to handle. To say that I was ready to give up is perhaps an understatement. I stopped cooking, and, frankly, I stopped even trying.

But then Frank, began to push me to work on *Italian Moms*. At first, it was a way for us to spend time together, and as the stories of my life were put down on paper, the book was transformed into a family legacy project—equal parts memoir and recipe collection. Then, after more than eight hundred strangers reached out to sponsor a crowd-funding page we had started on the Internet, working on the cookbook became a way to pay back the kindness of strangers. Over time, obligation morphed into joy as the tone of the stories I told my son changed from sadness to funny anecdotes and happy reflections on a life spent with my love and best friend, Francesco. Even if the book had never been published, the ability to relive those stories would have sufficed to make all the work worthwhile.

But then the book *was* published, and, oh, how the blessings rolled in! The process of working on it helped heal my aching heart, but little did I know that these were only the first steps in my journey. As we waited for the books to arrive, a school approached us to help with an event. The name of that school, St. Francis de Salles School, was too similar to my late husband's, Francesco, to ignore that good things were on the way. That simple request led to several more, including many unexpected opportunities, like an invitation to teach cooking classes in Tuscany. Over the months, as our mailbox filled with an increasing number of requests for recipes, general well wishes, and compliments for inspiring other seniors to be active and not give up, I felt reborn. A great many of these letters expressed thanks for preserving the almost lost art of cooking. Countless people told me that they wished they had collected their mothers' and grandmothers' recipes before they passed. At last, and most unexpectedly, I had found a new purpose for my life.

When the opportunity to put together a second cookbook came around, it all seemed less strange and more purposeful. As I started to gather recipes to include, I found myself reflecting again on the idea of looking backward to find the inspiration to journey forward, to honor tradition while embarking on the unknown journey that is life. I feel I have learned a great deal since the first *Italian Moms*. This time, there was much less kicking and screaming during the process, and I actually appreciated the chance to once again share my version of home cooking, influenced by my childhood in Abruzzi.

The book you now hold in your hands, *Italian Moms: Something Old, Something New*, celebrates the past while also paying homage to the newer generations of Italian-Americans who have rein-vented the classic recipes. Among the inspirations for the material in this book are my children, who have adapted my recipes as they have fed their own families over the years. This, to me, is the essence of legacy. The lessons I taught my children now are being passed on to future generations, perhaps modernized and adapted along the way to suit the times.

What this represents most of all is the timelessness of family, and, in some small way, it extends my time on earth. The idea of my son and daughter in the kitchen with their own children fills me with a joy and happiness that I cannot express. And to think that some small part of me—maybe the way I taught them to prepare pasta or bake bread—will live on as they spread their art to every table!

Not too long ago, I thought I was living the final chapter of my life. Little did I know that I had so much more to share and many, many chapters yet to live. I dedicate this book, once again, to the memory of my daughter, Agnes, who left this world too soon. Most of all, I celebrate all the moments that have been part of my life, as each and every one of them has helped build the tradition I pass along to the future.

Something old and something new, indeed!

Chapter One
ANTIPASTI

ABOARD THE SS *INDEPENDENCE*: MY FIRST GLIMPSES AT AMERICAN LIFE

n August 1961, after five months of paperwork, I boarded the SS *Independence* in the port town of Napoli, Italy, to start a new life in America. I wore a pretty new dress that my father had saved to buy for me. The gift meant a great deal, for although he understood Francesco's desire to move to America, my father was not exactly sure we were doing the right thing. Buying me a new dress, then, was his way of saying that he wanted me, his sole surviving daughter, to feel special and cared for wherever I lived.

The voyage, from Napoli to New York, was to take ten days. My parents dutifully carried my scant luggage—a small trunk of linens and my clothes—onto the ship for me. Most of the clothes were given to me by my cousin, Pierina, who already lived in the States and had returned to Italy for a visit. She said I would look more American, and hopefully, be spared the snub of the first-class passengers with these new things. She even tried to teach me some simple English phrases to get by. I also carried *una lira per un cocomero*, a lira my mother had given to me to purchase watermelon, one of my favorite treats, on the boat. Like my new dress, this was my mother's way of sending me off with something beyond her humble means to ensure that I felt special.

I was assigned to a tiny room on one of the ship's lower decks. The upper portion of the SS *Independence* was reserved for first-class passengers only; as I would come to find out, the luxuries of their journey afforded them an entirely different transatlantic experience. Nevertheless, my roommate for the trip was a pretty girl of seventeen years named Carmelina. The instant my father laid eyes on her, I could tell that he did not approve; she was single and vibrant, with a *joie de vive* that I am sure he recognized in himself. True to form, during the voyage, Carmelina very much enjoyed the party-like atmosphere on the ship.

Each night, many immigrants onboard would gather to dance and sing the night away. Unlike me, they seemed happy and excited about what America could mean for them. I had a much different mind-set about the trip and where I was going to eventually end up. I was alone, forced to leave Francesco and my daughter Nadia behind. At the time, I did not know when I would get to see them again. And so, I occupied myself and stayed busy to distract myself from the fears and doubts filling my head. Every morning, I went to the chapel to pray and seek guidance. It was there that I heard about the Cuban missile crisis. I could not pretend to understand all that was going on, but it sounded ominous and scary, and it only compounded my anxiety.

Aside from Carmelina, I made friends with two other women on the ship. One of them had left her dying mother behind, a fact that amazed me, but made me realize the sacrifices that people were willing to make to move to America. We spent a lot of time together, talking about the old country and wondering about our futures. Each day, I also spent time writing letters to my Francesco, intending to drop the entire bundle into a mailbox as soon as we arrived in America.

In addition to the impromptu parties the passengers hosted each night, there also were performances and plays arranged by the ship's crew. There was a swimming pool on the ship, too, but it was only available to those in first class. The rest of us stayed below deck the entire voyage, with the exception of one day when the waters were particularly rough and all passengers were taken to the pool deck. So, I did get to see my first swimming pool. Seeing how those in first class traveled was the first hint that life would be different for me in America. As an immigrant, I now realized that I would have a completely different experience because of my situation in life.

But even on the lower decks, I got a sense of the abundance that is part of life in America. In our village, we ate according to whatever was being harvested from the earth. We would not dare to waste even the most basic vegetable because it was all we had. Small portions and careful cooking were essential to preserving our supplies. Using gentle techniques and moderate cooking temperatures might have meant it took longer to prepare a meal, but it also meant we were being careful not to ruin our precious foods.

On the SS *Independence,* I was able to try a great many new foods. For example, this was the first time I ever ate pancakes and waffles. I had never had syrup before, either. In fact, breakfast was a very big deal on the ship—probably having something to do with the fact that everybody had been up late the night before dancing and partying. For the first time in my life, I saw a buffet with long rows of assorted food items: tray after tray of breakfast meats, scrambled eggs, bread, toast, fruits and vegetables, cheeses, and oatmeal (something else I had never laid eyes on). The sheer quantity of food served at every meal was massive, and I just could not get over how much of it there was. And, at the end of each meal service, there were still heaps of food remaining. It was both extraordinary and appalling to my naive sensibilities.

My favorite new food on the ship was rice pudding. I had never tasted this particular delicacy before, but, from the first spoonful, I was in love with its creamy texture and hints of cinnamon. I also learned that I very much liked a nice steak, cooked rare, something that would have been luxury item in Italy. Not all the food appealed to me, however. The pasta, cooked in extremely large quantities, was waterlogged and mushy. To my taste, it was an abomination, an abuse of the simple pasta that we would have taken great care to make. It was also covered in a generic, plain-tasting sauce. Cooked ham and macaroni and cheese were also completely new to me. I thought the ham would be at least similar to the pancetta that I was used to. Safe to say, it was not at all what I expected. I found the macaroni and cheese to be an odd mix of sloppy pasta and bland, plastic-like cheese. Fortunately, I have come to find out that there are much better ways to prepare macaroni and cheese, but, at the time, I was simply unimpressed by the gloopy yellow macaroni elbows. I managed to gain four pounds on the voyage but wasn't worried because I thought I'd have time to lose it before Francesco arrived in America.

Aside from the food, the journey felt like the longest ten days of my life. On the last day, the crew allowed us access to the upper deck, and, if I try, I can still recall the smell of the salt in the air, my first real experience of fresh air after being confined to the lower decks. I also remember clearly my first glimpse of America. As the sun was rising, I stood peering out over the bow just as our ship roared toward New York harbor. Off in the distance, the Statue of Liberty came into view, setting off cheering and celebration all around. But I remained locked in place, my eyes fixed on this tremendous statue of a lady holding a torch to the sky, a beacon welcoming us to a new world.

As lovely as this scene was, my joy was quickly dashed as our ship slumped to the dock. I looked along the shoreline and could make out the rows upon rows of homes, stacked together like boxes. They looked like train cars to me, each one identical to the one next to

it. There was no space between the houses and it seemed like everyone lived on top of one another in one massive cluster. At that moment, and for a long time after, I would yearn for the fields and expansive space of my little village.

When I finally disembarked, my brother Joe was there waiting for me. Because I had longed to see a familiar face, as soon as I saw him, I started to recount all the stories of my strange adventure. I told him, over and over, that I could not wait to see Francesco and did not know when we would be together again. Joe smiled each time I said this. He knew something I did not, and finally, he let me in on his secret.

In fact, Francesco and Nadia's paperwork had been approved while I was crossing the Atlantic, and Francesco had booked airfare for himself and Nadia, hoping to arrive before me as a surprise. The speed of the SS *Independence* spoiled his plan, as we arrived a day early. I had explicitly told Francesco that he should never travel in an airplane; I had never flown, and the thought of it scared me. But without me knowing it, Francesco had wished me well on my voyage, saw me off to the *SS Independence,* and had already planned to shorten our separation with a plane ride, as soon as he could.

I should have been furious, but I was not. In fact, I was so elated at the idea of seeing my family again that I tossed the bundle of letters I held clutched in my hands, yelled to my ship friends in excitement, and began to run to Joe's car, as if speeding up this part of our journey would somehow reunite us sooner. I never exchanged addresses with these women, which I regret, as I would love to know how they are and what kind of life they made for themselves. Joe and I still had a two- or three-hour drive to Philadelphia ahead of us, but this fact did not matter to me. My heart was in my throat, and I did not realize until about an hour later that I had lost the letters I had written while on the ship.

That night I sat at dinner with Joe and Pierina and with Francesco and Nadia by my side. It was a simple meal. We ate chicken and rice, hardly a fancy thing to eat. But, at that point and time, and after such a long voyage, it was perhaps one of the most memorable meals of my young life. Never before and never again would simple chicken and rice taste so delicious and be so fulfilling.

"My wife and I enjoy entertaining; however, most of Mom's traditional antipasti dishes require a sit-down setting. These antipasti recipes are a combination of Abruzzo classics, as well as some adaptations of Mom's classic dishes—all reinvented for casual gatherings and to accommodate the busy schedules of the modern family. We believe they make the perfect cocktail party treats, and we hope you enjoy them as much as we do!"

—FRANK

CRÊPE BITES

(Scrippelle Arrotolate)

Serves 6–8 people

For the crêpes:

5 jumbo eggs

1¼ cups all-purpose flour

½ cup olive oil

For the filling:

2 16-ounce containers of cream cheese

1 pound prosciutto, sliced thin

Directions

1. *Prepare the crêpes:* Beat the eggs in the bowl of an electric stand mixer, fitted with a beater attachment, then gradually sift in the flour. Continue to beat at a very low speed for 5–10 minutes, while gradually adding 1¾ cups of water. Continue to beat until the batter is very smooth, with no visible lumps.

2. Heat an 8- or 10-inch nonstick pan over low heat. (You must use a nonstick pan to keep the crêpes from burning and sticking to the pan. I use a 10-inch pan that yields 10–15 crêpes.) Put the olive oil in a small bowl. Dip a paper towel into the olive oil and grease the pan; you will need to repeat the greasing of the pan after every three or four crêpes. Using a ladle, spread the batter lightly to cover the entire diameter of the pan. Allow the crêpe to cook for 2–3 minutes, then remove with a fork and transfer to a paper towel–covered work surface. Add some water to the batter if it becomes too thick and does not run easily over the pan. Line the finished crêpes on paper towels (do not stack them) until ready to use.

3. *Fill and roll the crêpes, one at a time:* Once the crêpes are cool, spread a generous amount of cream cheese over the crêpe, then add slices of the prosciutto to cover. Roll the crêpe tightly and place on a large platter. When all the crêpes are rolled, cover with plastic wrap and refrigerate for 1 hour.

4. Using a sharp knife, cut off the rounded edges. Slice the rolls into ½-inch pieces. Arrange on a platter and serve.

FRIED VEGETABLES

(Verdure Miste Fritte)

Serves 4–6 people

Ingredients

1 cauliflower head, cut into florets

1 broccoli head, cut into florets

1 eggplant, peeled and sliced

1 zucchini, peeled and sliced

2 large eggs

1 cup all-purpose flour

1 tablespoon baking powder

1 cup club soda

Vegetable oil, for frying

Directions

1. Place the cauliflower and broccoli florets in a saucepan of water, bring to a boil, and boil for 5 minutes. Remove and drain on a paper towel–lined wire rack.

2. Beat the eggs in a large mixing bowl. Add the flour, baking powder, and club soda, and whisk together to create a consistent batter.

3. Heat the vegetable oil in a large frying pan over medium heat. Dip each vegetable piece into the batter, shaking off excess, and place in the hot oil. Dip and fry several pieces in batches (do not overcrowd the pan), for 3–4 minutes, until brown. Remove and cool on a wire rack. Arrange on a serving platter and serve.

CHEESE PUFFS

(Fiadoni)

Serves 4–6 people

Ingredients

For the filling:

½ cup freshly grated Parmesan cheese

½ cup freshly grated Pecorino Romano cheese

½ cup Ricotta cheese, drained

Pinch of salt and black pepper

2 tablespoons grated black truffles (if available; can be omitted)

For the pastry:

2 cups all-purpose flour

1 teaspoon baking powder

2 large eggs

¼ cup lard or other solid shortening, cut into little pieces

¼ cup olive oil

¼ cup dry white wine

Directions

1. Preheat the oven to 350°F.

2. *Prepare the filling:* Mix together the cheeses, salt, pepper, and truffle in a glass bowl. Refrigerate mixture, covered with plastic wrap, until ready to use.

3. *Prepare the pastry:* Sift the flour and baking powder into a mound on a wooden or marble-type surface. Hollow the center of the mound with a spoon. Place 1 egg, the lard, oil, and wine in a bowl, and mix thoroughly, then add the mixture to the well. Incorporate the flour and liquid mixture until you have a solid dough. Knead the dough for 10–15 minutes, until smooth and silky.

4. Divide the dough into two equal parts and roll out the dough with the pasta machine until you reach the thinnest notch (in the same way that you would make ravioli). Place small heaps of filling, 3 inches apart, on one of the rolled strips and cover with the other rolled strip.

"*Fiadoni*, another treasure from Abruzzo, can be found throughout the region during the Easter season. For those who produce fresh goat cheese, these treats are served all year round, especially for family celebrations. Although my hometown prefers to add fresh truffle shavings found on our neighboring hillsides, others add cured meat, like pancetta, or mint or saffron. If working with homemade dough is beyond your comfort zone, frozen puff pastry sheets work just as well."

—ELISA

5. Cut *fiadoni* with a ravioli cutter in the shape of a crescent. Press the dough edges together firmly with a fork. Cut a small cross along the top of each *fiadoni* to allow the pastry to breathe.

6. Beat the remaining egg in a small bowl and, using a pastry brush, brush the *fiadoni* with the egg.

7. Place *fiadoni*, 3 inches apart, on a greased or parchment paper–lined baking sheet and bake for 15 minutes, or until golden brown. Remove from oven and transfer to a wire rack. Cool slightly for 2–3 minutes. Serve warm.

NOTE

To knead the dough, you may use a food processor, set to the dough feature,
or an electric stand mixer, fitted with a kneading attachment.

AVOCADO AND GOAT CHEESE DIP

(Tuffato in Formaggio di Capra)

Serves 4 people

Ingredients

4 avocados

2 cups goat cheese

1 cup Gorgonzola cheese

2 garlic cloves, chopped

¼ cup chopped parsley

Toasted bread, for serving

Directions

Slice avocados in half, discard the pit, and spoon out the flesh into a bowl. Add the cheeses, garlic, and parsley and mix thoroughly. Chill in the refrigerator for 1 hour. Serve with toasted bread.

"When we were young and the late summer brought many figs, we would make this dip to spread on toasted bread with figs. Since figs are harder to obtain here in the States, my brother often substitutes avocados for the figs."

—ELISA

RED PEPPER FRITTATA

(Frittata al Pepe Rosso)

Serves 4 people

Ingredients

¼ cup olive oil, plus 1 tablespoon

4 red roasting peppers, chopped

Salt and black pepper, to taste

8 eggs

1 cup chopped onions

¼ cup grated Pecorino
Romano cheese

Directions

1. Heat ¼ cup of olive oil in a sauté pan over medium heat. Add the red peppers and a pinch of salt and sauté for 10–15 minutes, until tender.

2. Beat the eggs in a glass mixing bowl. Pour 1 tablespoon of olive oil onto a paper towel and grease a 10- or 12-inch nonstick pan with a heavy bottom and rounded edges. Heat the pan over medium heat for 2–3 minutes. Pour the beaten eggs into the pan and add the red peppers and onions. Gently mix before the eggs begin to cook. Sprinkle half the cheese over the eggs and add a pinch of salt and black pepper, then cook, undisturbed, until firm. Flip the frittata over and sprinkle with the remaining cheese and another pinch of salt and pepper. Cook for an additional 2–3 minutes. Remove from pan and slice into wedges. Serve warm or cold.

POTATO AND ONION FRITTATA

(Frittata di Patate e Cipolla)

Serves 4 people

Ingredients

2 russet potatoes, peeled and cut into ¼ -inch-thick slices

¼ cup olive oil

1 medium Spanish onion, chopped

¼ cup finely chopped fresh parsley

1 teaspoon chopped fresh rosemary, plus more for garnish

2 pinches salt and chili pepper

6 large eggs

¼ cup freshly grated Parmesan cheese, plus more for garnish

¼ cup whole milk

Toasted bread, for serving

Directions

1. Bring a small saucepan of water to a boil. Place sliced potatoes in boiling water and boil for 5–7 minutes. Remove and arrange on a paper towel.

2. Heat olive oil in a 10-inch frying pan over medium-high heat. Add the onions and boiled potatoes and sauté for 2–3 minutes. Add the parsley, rosemary, and a pinch of salt and chili pepper, and sauté for an additional 2–3 minutes.

3. Beat the eggs, half of the cheese, and the milk in a glass bowl and slowly add to the onions and potatoes. Gently mix before eggs begin to cook, then cook, undisturbed, until firm. Flip the frittata over and sprinkle with the remaining cheese and another pinch of salt and chili pepper.

4. Cook for an additional 2–3 minutes. Remove from the pan and slice into wedges. Garnish with some additional cheese and rosemary. Serve warm or cold, with some warm toasted bread.

MINT PANCAKES

(Frittelle di Menta)

Makes 1 dozen pancakes

Ingredients

1 ¼ cups whole-wheat flour

½ teaspoon baking powder

2 large eggs

⅔ cup whole milk

¼ cup olive oil

Pinch of salt

1 cup chopped fresh mint

2 tablespoons butter

Directions

1. Into a large mixing bowl, sift the flour and baking powder. Add the eggs and beat until combined. Add the milk, ⅓ cup of cold water, olive oil, and salt, and whisk to a smooth consistency. Add the mint and mix thoroughly. Refrigerate for at least 1 hour, and up to 10 hours.

2. Melt the butter in a large sauté pan over medium heat. Add a small ladleful of batter, the size of a silver dollar pancake, and tilt the batter in the pan to flatten it slightly. When the ends become firm, flip over and cook for another 30 seconds. Total cooking time per pancake should be 2 minutes. Remove from heat. Fold pancakes in half and arrange on a serving dish with some cranberry sauce. Serve warm.

THE HISTORY OR MYTH OF MINT IN ABRUZZO

had forgotten just how much wild mint could be found throughout my village and along the roads leading to the mountains until my last visit home this past summer. As I was walking with Zia Maria Costantini, my late husband's only living aunt, she reminded me of the folktale of Ovid. Ovid, an ancient storyteller, told the story of Myntha, a beautiful woman, who was desired by many men, including Pluto, and hated by all the women. One of those women was Proserpina, the jealous wife of Pluto, who decided to place Myntha under a spell. Being the goddess of the harvest, Proserpina changed Myntha into the form of a plant that would grow along open paths, hoping that she would be trampled on. Pluto, determined to show his devotion and to ensure that his love was not destroyed, gave the plant its aroma, hoping it would draw people to the plant, rather than destroy it. His plan worked, and as people discovered the plant, they began to flavor their water with it and to incorporate it into their cooking; they even placed it in their undergarments. Zia Maria told me that many brides would add mint to their bouquets on their wedding day because of the fresh fragrance. The myth also suggests that as new love spread among young couples, so did the plants, filling the countryside with the aroma of the love of the gods.

BROCCOLI FRITTATA CUPS

(Frittata di Broccoli)

Makes 2 dozen cups

Ingredients

3 cups fresh broccoli florets

1 tablespoon olive oil, plus more for greasing the muffin tin

1 cup cubed pancetta (optional)

1 Spanish onion, chopped

2 cloves garlic, minced

4 jumbo eggs

¼ cup freshly grated Parmesan cheese

¼ cup freshly grated Pecorino Romano cheese, plus more for topping

½ cup freshly grated Friulano or mild cheddar cheese

¼ cup finely chopped fresh parsley

¼ cup whole milk

Pinch of salt and black pepper

Directions

1. Preheat the oven to 400°F. Grease thoroughly two 12-cup mini muffin tins or one 24-cup mini muffin tin.

2. Place broccoli florets in a saucepan and cover with water. Bring to a boil and cook for 3–4 minutes. Remove from the heat and drain well. Once the broccoli is cool, chop into smaller pieces.

3. Heat the olive oil in a skillet over medium heat and sauté pancetta for 2 minutes. Add the onion and garlic, and sauté for an additional 5 minutes. Remove from heat and drain any grease. In a large mixing bowl, beat the eggs, and stir in the broccoli, cheeses, parsley, milk, salt, and pepper. Fold in the sautéed pancetta and onions.

4. Spoon the batter into the muffin tins, filling them halfway. Top with some more grated cheese, salt, and pepper.

5. Bake for 12–14 minutes, or until golden brown. Remove from the oven and allow to cool for a few minutes. Using a knife, gently remove the frittata cups from the muffin tin and arrange them on a serving platter. Serve warm or cold.

NOTE

You can use paper muffin liners instead of greasing the muffin tins, if you like.

"On any given morning for breakfast, or for midday, packed in our lunchbox, or even as part of our dinner, Mom would prepare frittatas. Depending on the time of year, it could be prepared with cured meats from the winter, cheeses brought over from Italy by relatives, or fresh vegetables from the garden. We have taken Mom's classic frittata recipe and created a perfect bite-size cocktail party treat. This recipe allows you to incorporate any of Mom's other frittata specialties."

—FRANK

FRIED MOZZARELLA

(Mozzarella Fritta)

Serves 4–6 people

Ingredients

8 ounces fresh
Mozzarella cheese

3 eggs

Salt and black pepper, to taste

4 cups Italian breadcrumbs

Vegetable oil, for frying

Marinara sauce, for serving

Directions

1. Drain the mozzarella and cut it into ¼-inch slices. Line a colander with the slices and place paper towels underneath the colander to absorb any liquid that drains out. (This is one of the secrets to frying cheese). Refrigerate for 1 hour.

2. Whisk the eggs and a pinch of salt and pepper in a bowl. Pour breadcrumbs into a separate bowl large enough to hold a slice of cheese.

3. Working with one slice of cheese at a time, dip cheese into the eggs, coating both sides, then place in the breadcrumbs and flip a few times to evenly cover both sides. Shake off any excess, then dip into the eggs and breadcrumbs again. Place the coated slice on a plate. Repeat this procedure for each piece of cheese. (This double coating is the second secret to frying cheese.)

4. Add enough oil to a large sauté pan to ensure that the cheese slices will be covered when frying them, then heat the oil over medium heat. Place a few slices into the oil (do not overcrowd the pan) and fry for 3–5 minutes on each side, until lightly browned. Remove from the pan and place on a paper towel–covered plate to absorb the excess oil. Transfer to a serving platter. Continue to fry and drain the remaining cheese in the same way. Serve with some marinara sauce for dipping.

"For years we asked Mom to make us fried Mozzarella, and she always said no. After several failed attempts on my own, I accepted the fact that this would be a treat I only enjoyed while dining out. Then, one day, we arrived at her house for Sunday dinner. As usual, she had some cutlets, roasted peppers, fresh bread, and cheese waiting for us to nibble on until dinner was ready. But this time the cheese was fried. It wasn't Mozzarella, but rather a soft, creamy cheese we had brought back from the Gran Sasso Mountains the previous summer. I turned to Mom and asked her, if she could fry this cheese, then why not the Mozzarella? She paused, raised her wooden spoon, and calmly said, I guess we can. But you need to know the secrets to frying cheese. I guess the moral of this story is that all good things come to those who wait, and no one can tell Italian mothers what to do in the kitchen; they say how, and they say when!"

—FRANK

CHEESE AND ONION CROSTINI, "SHEPHERD'S STEAK"

(Bistecca del Lavoratore con Crostini di Formaggio e Cipolla)

Serves 4 people

Ingredients

8 slices day-old or stale Italian bread (see Notes below)

1 cup heavy cream or whole milk

Pinch of salt and black pepper

2 red onions, thinly sliced

1 pound Pecorino Romano cheese, cut into ¼-inch-thick slices (see Notes)

Fresh mint leaves

Directions

1. Preheat the oven to 350°F.

2. Slice the bread into ½-inch slices. Pour the cream, salt, and pepper into a shallow bowl large enough to cover the slices of bread, and mix thoroughly. Soak the slices of bread in the cream. Place the soaked bread on a nonstick or parchment–lined baking sheet.

3. Arrange the slices of onions on top of the bread and place a slice of the cheese over the onions.

4. Bake for 10–12 minutes, until cheese has melted. Add additional pepper, garnish with fresh mint, and serve.

NOTES

If you do not have stale bread, toast your bread on a light setting so it is firm enough to hold the milk. Any sheep's milk cheese can be used in this recipe.

ANCHOVY CROSTINI

(Crostini di Scamorza e Alici)

Serves 4 people

Ingredients

8 slices day-old or stale
Italian bread

1 cup heavy cream or whole milk

Pinch of salt and black pepper

$^3/_4$ pound fresh Scamorza or
Mozzarella cheese, cut into
$^1/_4$-inch-thick slices

24 anchovy fillets

Directions

1. Preheat the oven to 350°F.

2. Slice the bread into ½-inch slices. Pour the cream, salt, and pepper into a shallow bowl large enough to cover the slices of bread, and mix thoroughly. Soak the slices of bread in the cream. Place the soaked bread on a nonstick or parchment–lined baking sheet.

3. Arrange a slice of cheese on each piece of bread and top each with 3 anchovy fillets.

4. Bake for 5–7 minutes, until cheese has melted. Sprinkle with salt and pepper, and serve.

NOTE
*If you do not have stale bread, toast bread on a light
setting so it is firm enough to hold the milk.*

SAUSAGE CROSTINI

(Crostini di Salsiccia)

Ingredients

8 slices Italian bread

½ pound sausage preserves,
or fresh Italian sausage, crumbled

Olive oil

Pinch of salt and black pepper

1 tablespoon lard (if using fresh sausage)

Directions

1. Preheat the oven to 350°F.

2. If using sausage preserves, slice bread into ½-inch slices and toast in the oven for 2–3 minutes. Spread sausage preserves over slices of bread. Drizzle with olive oil, add a pinch of salt and pepper, and serve.

3. If using fresh sausage, do not pre-toast your bread. Heat a tablespoon of olive oil in a medium sauté pan, then add crumbled sausage and sauté for 4–5 minutes. Drain sausage and place on a paper towel to drain any additional grease. Allow the sausage to cool. Place sausage in a bowl with a tablespoon of lard and mix thoroughly. Spread the sausage mixture over the sliced bread and add a pinch of salt and pepper. Place the slices of bread on a nonstick or parchment–lined baking sheet. Bake for 5–6 minutes, until the bread is lightly toasted and serve.

"During the first week of February, my brother Nicola and I prepare fresh sausage for the family. Although we dry out most of the sausage to be used over a few months' time, we preserve some in salt, fat, and oil to be used for this amazing sausage spread. This sausage spread may be found in some Italian specialty shops, but if you cannot find it, you can use fresh-cooked sausage as well."

—ELISA

ROASTED ARTICHOKE CROSTINI

(Crostini di Carciofi Arrosto)

Serves 4 people

Ingredients

12 slices Italian bread

1 (14-ounce) can artichoke hearts, drained

¼ cup olive oil

4 garlic cloves, chopped

Pinch of salt and black pepper

¼ cup freshly grated Parmesan or Pecorino Romano cheese

¼ cup chopped fresh parsley, for garnish

Directions

1. Preheat the oven to 350°F.

2. Slice bread into ½-inch slices and toast in oven for 2–3 minutes. Set aside.

3. Increase oven temperature to 425°F. Drain the artichoke hearts and place in a large mixing bowl. Add olive oil, garlic, salt, and pepper, and toss thoroughly. Arrange artichokes in one layer on a parchment-lined baking sheet. Bake for 10 minutes. Remove from the oven and sprinkle artichokes with grated cheese. Bake an additional 5 minutes, until cheese melts. Remove from the oven and spread artichokes over the toasted bread slices. Garnish with chopped parsley and serve warm.

FRIED CELERY

(Sedano Fritto)

Ingredients

3 cups vegetable oil

4 celery stalks
(see Note below)

6 eggs, separated

Pinch of salt and black pepper

3 cups all-purpose flour

Juice of 1 lemon

2 tablespoons white vinegar

2 tablespoons freshly grated
Pecorino Romano cheese

Directions

1. Heat the oil in a large frying pan over medium heat while you prepare the celery.

2. Wash the celery under cold water and dry. Cut celery stalks into three even pieces. Beat 3 of the egg yolks, salt, and pepper in a bowl. Place the flour in another bowl. Dip each piece of celery into the egg yolks, then dredge in the flour, coating evenly on all sides. Shake off any excess flour, then dip into the eggs and flour again.

3. Place the coated celery sticks in the hot oil (do not overcrowd the pan) and fry, turning occasionally, until the batter is golden brown. Remove sticks from the oil and drain on a paper towel–lined wire rack to drain any excess oil.

4. In a small pot, place 3 egg whites, lemon juice, and vinegar and beat thoroughly. Cook over low heat, stirring continuously, for 3–4 minutes. Add the cheese and continue to stir until the sauce thickens.

5. Arrange the celery on a platter and drizzle with the sauce, or serve the sauce in a small serving bowl for dipping.

NOTE

You can use precut, packaged celery sticks to save time.

PANCETTA CORN CAKES

(Frittelle di Mais con Pancetta)

Makes 8–10 cakes

1 cup frozen corn kernels, thawed to room
temperature and drained

1 cup cubed pancetta

1 Spanish onion, chopped

2 eggs, separated

$1/2$ cup freshly grated
Parmesan cheese

$1/4$ cup heavy cream

3 cups flour

1 teaspoon salt

1 teaspoon black pepper

1 teaspoon hot red pepper

3 cups vegetable oil

Freshly grated Pecorino
Romano cheese, for garnish

1. Place corn kernels in a bowl of hot water and set aside for 30 minutes. Remove and drain well.

2. In a large mixing bowl, combine corn, pancetta, onion, egg yolks, Parmesan cheese, and heavy cream, and mix thoroughly. In another bowl, combine 1 cup of the flour, salt, black pepper, and hot red pepper. In a third bowl, beat the egg whites thoroughly with a handheld electric mixer. Add the flour mixture to the corn mixture and blend thoroughly with a wooden spoon. Fold in the egg whites, then refrigerate, covered with plastic wrap, for 1 hour.

3. Heat the oil in a medium saucepan over medium heat. Place the remaining 2 cups of flour in a small bowl.

4. Take $1\frac{1}{2}$ tablespoons of the chilled corn mixture at a time and form into a ball. Roll it in the flour, flatten the ball, and set aside. Form all the corn cakes with the remaining corn mixture in the same way.

5. Add 2–3 cakes at a time to the hot oil (do not overcrowd the pan) and fry, in batches, for 4–5 minutes, turning occasionally, until golden brown. As fried, remove the cakes from the oil and place on a wire rack to drain any excess oil. Add a pinch of salt and garnish with Pecorino Romano cheese. Arrange on a serving platter and serve.

POTATO PROSCIUTTO BISCUITS

(Biscotti di Patate e Prosciutto)

Makes 1 dozen biscuits

Ingredients

1 cup mashed potatoes

Pinch of salt

2 tablespoons freshly grated Parmesan or Pecorino Romano cheese

1½ cups all-purpose flour, plus more for dusting

3 tablespoons butter, cubed

3 teaspoons baking powder

½ cup whole milk

3–4 slices prosciutto, thinly sliced and finely chopped

3–4 slices Provolone or sharp Italian cheese, thinly sliced and chopped

1 egg

¼ cup heavy cream

Directions

1. Place the mashed potatoes in a large mixing bowl. Add the salt, grated cheese, flour, butter, and baking powder, and mix thoroughly. Then slowly add the milk. Knead the dough until it's a uniform consistency. Add the chopped prosciutto and Provolone cheese and knead in thoroughly. Form the dough into a ball, wrap with plastic wrap, and refrigerate for 30 minutes.

2. Preheat the oven to 450°F.

3. Roll out the dough onto a floured surface with a rolling pin. Using a biscuit cutter or a small glass, cut out the biscuits. Arrange the biscuits 1 inch apart on a parchment-lined baking sheet or a greased cast-iron biscuit pan. Place the egg and the heavy cream in a small bowl and whisk together to make an egg wash; brush biscuits with the egg wash.

4. Bake for 10–15 minutes, or until golden brown. (The biscuits will remain somewhat flat.) Transfer to a serving platter and serve.

"This was a traditional afternoon snack usually prepared when gnocchi were made for lunch. Since the potatoes for these biscuits are prepared in the same way you would prepare gnocchi, it just required making extra potatoes. The men would take these biscuits back to work with them and have them as their *merenda* (snack) in the late afternoon before returning home after a long day at work."

—ELISA

BROCCOLI BITES

(Polpettine di Broccoli)

Serves 4–6 people

Ingredients

2 cups fresh broccoli florets

6 eggs

3 cups Italian breadcrumbs

½ cup freshly grated
Parmesan cheese

½ cup freshly grated Pecorino
Romano cheese

Pinch of salt and black pepper

Pinch of red pepper powder

2 garlic cloves, minced

1 tablespoon finely chopped fresh
oregano

¼ cup finely chopped
fresh parsley

Roasted Red Pepper Cream
Spread (page 227), for serving

Directions

1. Place the broccoli florets in a saucepan and cover with water. Bring to a boil and cook for 3–4 minutes. Remove from heat and drain well. Once the broccoli cools, chop it into smaller pieces.

2. In a bowl, beat the eggs, then add the breadcrumbs, cheeses, and broccoli, and mix together. Add salt, black and red peppers, garlic, oregano, and parsley, and mix thoroughly. Take 1 teaspoon of the mixture, form it into a ball the size of an olive, and place it on a nonstick or parchment-lined baking sheet. Make more balls with the remaining mixture in the same way and refrigerate, covered with plastic wrap, for 1 hour.

3. Preheat the oven to 350°F.

4. Bake broccoli bites for 15–20 minutes, until golden brown. Remove from the oven and arrange on a serving tray. Serve warm with a side of my Roasted Red Pepper Cream Spread.

"Create something new from something old. Here we have taken Mom's *Abruzzese Polpettine,* or cheese balls, from *Italian Moms— Spreading Their Art to Every Table,* and added something new. These delicious bursts of flavor are sure to be well received by your guests. We also chose to bake them instead of using the traditional frying method."

—FRANK

SPINACH AND ONION ARANCINI

(Arancini di Spinaci e Cipolla)

Ingredients

2 cups cooked risotto

1 (10-ounce) package frozen chopped
spinach, thawed

1 small onion, finely chopped

½ cup freshly grated Pecorino
Romano cheese

½ cup freshly grated
Mozzarella cheese

½ cup freshly grated
Parmesan cheese

3 eggs

Pinch of salt and black pepper

1 cup Italian breadcrumbs

4 cups vegetable oil, for frying

Warm marinara sauce, for serving

Directions

1. Prepare the risotto a day before preparing the arancini.

2. Drain the spinach well, and squeeze dry between layers of paper towels. Combine risotto, spinach, onion, cheeses, 1 egg, salt, and pepper in a large mixing bowl, and use your hands to thoroughly combine the mixture. Form each arancini by taking a small portion of the mixture, about the size of a small orange, and squeezing it firmly into a nice round shape. Form approximately 7 more arancini in the same way.

3. In a bowl, whisk together the remaining 2 eggs. Put the breadcrumbs in another bowl. Roll each arancini in the egg, then roll in the breadcrumbs, shaking off any excess. Put the arancini on a plate and refrigerate for 15–20 minutes.

4. Heat 4 inches of oil, enough to fully cover the arancini, in a saucepan over medium heat until hot. Reduce the heat slightly, then add 2 or 3 breaded arancini to the oil (do not overcrowd the pan) and fry, for 5–7 minutes, until golden brown and thoroughly cooked. Using a slotted spoon, remove the fried arancini and transfer to a paper towel–lined plate to drain. Fry the remaining arancini. Arrange arancini on a serving platter, and serve with warm marinara sauce.

NOTES

You can use a deep fryer instead of a saucepan.
You can bake the arancini, if you prefer. Preheat the oven to 400°F.
Arrange arancini on a nonstick baking sheet and bake for 20–25 minutes,
until golden brown.

WINE TARALLI

(Taralli al Vino)

Ingredients

4 cups all-purpose flour,
plus more for dusting

2 teaspoons baking powder

Pinch salt

3 eggs

1 cup sugar

½ cup vegetable oil

1 cup dry white wine

1 egg

¼ cup milk

"Create a wonderful antipasto by wrapping your taralli with some prosciutto and topping it with a green olive, Mozzarella ball, and cherry tomato."

—ELISA

Directions

1. Preheat the oven to 350°F.

2. In a large bowl, combine the flour, baking powder, and salt. Pour the flour mixture onto a clean wooden or marble-like surface and form a well in the center of the flour. In another mixing bowl, whisk together the eggs, sugar, oil, and wine, and pour the mixture into the flour well. Using your hands, fold the flour into the egg mixture until a dough is formed. Place the dough in a lightly floured bowl, cover, and set aside for 20 minutes.

3. Turn the dough out onto a lightly floured surface and knead for 3–4 minutes. Divide dough into four equal-sized pieces. Using the palms of your hands, roll each piece of dough into a rope, about 16 inches long. Cut the rope into four or five 4- to 6-inch lengths, depending on how large you like your taralli. Form each piece of dough into a circle and pinch the ends to secure the circle. Place the taralli 1 inch apart on a parchment-lined baking sheet. Place egg and milk in a small bowl and whisk together to make an egg wash; brush taralli with the egg wash.

4. Bake for 30–35 minutes, until lightly golden. Remove from the oven and place on a wire rack. Serve warm.

NOTES

You may also use an electric stand mixer, fitted with a kneading attachment, to form the dough. You can create larger taralli, if you like, but I prefer smaller, bite-size taralli.

HERB BREAD

(Pane alle Erbe)

Serves 4–6 people

Ingredients

6 ½ cups all-purpose flour, plus more for dusting

2 envelopes active dry yeast, or 2 teaspoons yeast

1 tablespoon salt

1 tablespoon dry basil

1 tablespoon dry oregano

1 teaspoon garlic powder

1 teaspoon onion powder

⅓ cup freshly grated Pecorino Romano cheese

¼ cup olive oil

Directions

1. In a small bowl, mix together 1 cup warm water, ½ cup flour, and the yeast, and allow to rest in a warm place for 30 minutes. On a clean wooden or marble-like surface, make a mound with the remaining 6 cups of flour and hollow out the center to create a well. Add 2 cups warm water, yeast mixture, salt, basil, oregano, garlic and onion powders, and cheese to the well, and whisk in the flour with a fork.

2. Once you have incorporated all the flour, knead the dough until it has a uniform consistency. Place the dough in an olive oil–greased bowl at least three times the size of the dough ball. Brush some olive oil on top of the dough and allow it to rise in a warm place, covered with a cloth, for 2–3 hours. Knead the dough again for 4–6 minutes, then return it to the bowl and cover. Allow the dough to rise for an additional hour.

3. Once the dough has risen and doubled in size, preheat the oven to 350°F.

4. Turn the dough out onto a lightly floured surface and knead it for 3–4 minutes. With a rolling pin, roll the dough into an oval shape, approximately three-fourths the length of a baking sheet. Place the dough on a greased baking sheet and allow it to rest for 10–15 minutes before placing it in oven.

5. Bake for 1 hour. Remove it from the oven, wrap it in a towel, and set it aside to cool.

PHILADELPHIA CHEESESTEAK STROMBOLI

(Stracceti di Carne al Formaggio in Crosta di Pane)

Serves 4–6 people

Ingredients

5 cups all-purpose flour

1 envelope active dry yeast

¼ cup olive oil, plus more for greasing and brushing

Pinch of salt and black pepper

2 teaspoons vegetable oil

2 small yellow onions, sliced

1 pound beef top round chipped steak

½ cup roasted red peppers

6–8 slices American cheese

6–8 slices Provolone cheese

¼ cup freshly grated Parmesan cheese

1 egg, beaten

Directions

1. In a small bowl, mix together ½ cup of warm water, ½ cup of flour, and the yeast, and allow the mixture to rest in a warm place for 30 minutes.

2. On a clean wooden or marble-like surface, make a mound with the remaining flour and hollow out the center with a spoon to make a well. Add 2 cups of warm water to the well and whisk with a fork. Add ¼ cup of olive oil, a pinch of salt, and the yeast mixture, and continue to whisk with a fork, gradually adding the flour from the mound. Once you have incorporated all the flour, knead well until the dough has a uniform consistency.

3. Place the dough in an olive oil–greased bowl at least three times the size of the dough ball. Brush some olive oil on top of the dough and set aside to rise in a warm place, covered with a cloth, for 2–3 hours.

4. While the dough is rising, heat the vegetable oil in a medium frying pan. Add the sliced onions and sauté for 5 minutes, then add the beef, salt, and black pepper, and cook for 10 minutes. Add the roasted red peppers and sauté for 2–3 minutes. Remove from heat and set aside.

5. Once the dough has risen, separate the dough into two equal-sized portions. Roll out each portion separately into a rectangular shape on a lightly floured surface. Divide the meat mixture and cheeses into two equal-sized parts. Working with one dough rectangle and one part of the filling at a time, line the top of the dough with a layer of meat, then the cheeses. Roll up the dough lengthwise, tightly. Fold over the ends and pinch tightly. Repeat with the second dough rectangle and filling.

6. Preheat the oven to 350°F. Then place the rolled stromboli, side by side, on an olive oil–greased baking sheet. Brush stromboli with the beaten egg and allow to rest on the sheet in the refrigerator for 10–15 minutes.

7. Bake for 30 minutes. Remove from the oven and cool for 20 minutes. Slice into 1½ - to 2-inch slices and serve.

RED PEPPER FOCACCIA BREAD

(Focaccia di Pepe Rosso)

Serves 4–6 people

Ingredients

5 cups all-purpose flour,
plus more for dusting

1 envelope active dry yeast or
1 teaspoon yeast

About ¼ cup olive oil

4–5 red roasting peppers,
cut into pieces

1 tablespoon salt

Directions

1. Mix together the flour, 2 cups of warm water, and the yeast in a large glass bowl. Set aside in a warm dry place and cover with a dishtowel. Allow to rise for 30–40 minutes.

2. Once the dough has risen, turn the dough out onto a floured surface and knead for 3–4 minutes. Add some flour if the dough is sticky. Place dough in an olive oil–greased bowl at least two times the size of the dough ball. Set aside, covered with a cloth in a warm place to rise for an additional 15–20 minutes.

3. Preheat the oven to 350°F.

4. Heat some olive oil in a sauté pan, then add the peppers and salt, and sauté for 5–7 minutes. Remove from heat and set aside.

5. Turn the dough out onto a floured surface and form the dough into an oval shape, approximately three-fourths the length of a baking sheet. Roll out dough to an even thickness and poke the dough all over with your fingertips. Grease the baking sheet with olive oil. Gently place the dough on the baking sheet and sprinkle the top with the remaining olive oil. Top with peppers.

6. Bake for 1 hour. Remove from the oven and cool on a wire rack.

For decades, celebrations in Italy have been surrounded by traditional meals with six to eight courses. What you may not know is that it is also traditional to feed your guests before the celebration even begins. It is customary to invite your party guests to your home prior to heading off to the church for the wedding ceremony, or christening, or whatever the celebration may be. And your guests will expect a little something to snack on. Traditionally, you would serve fresh-baked breads, cured meats, and cheeses you have made, and, of course, some biscotti. But over the years, younger generations have added a level of sophistication to the "pre-party" or "tailgate," as my grandson, Sebastian, calls it. An array of finger sandwiches and mini pizzas now grace the dining table for the guests to nibble on as they wait to wish a bride good luck, or congratulate the new parents on the day of their child's christening. Here are some of my family's favorites for these events. And, can you believe, after the formal celebration is over, many guests will return to your house and nibble on these favorites with their nightcap. What can I say? It isn't a successful celebration unless your guests have eaten at least three times before they go home!

TUNA AND CHILI PEPPER TEA SANDWICH

(Panino al Tonno e Peperoncino)

Serves 4–6 people

2 cans solid white tuna in olive oil

2 teaspoons red chili pepper spread, found at most deli counters

2 tablespoons mayonnaise

Pinch of salt

6–8 fresh bakery dinner rolls

Drain oil from tuna, and place tuna in a mixing bowl. Add the chili pepper spread, mayonnaise, and salt, and blend thoroughly. Slice rolls and fill with the desired amount of tuna mixture.

NOTE

LONZA AND TOMATO TEA SANDWICH

(Panino con Lonza e Pomodoro)

Serves 4–6 people

6–8 fresh bakery dinner rolls

12 to 16 $\frac{1}{8}$-inch slices of lonza (2 slices per sandwich: see Note below)

3–4 fresh tomatoes, sliced

Olive oil

Pinch of salt

¼ cup chopped fresh parsley

Slice rolls. Place two slices of lonza in each sandwich. Layer with a slice of tomato. Drizzle with a little olive oil and salt. Top with parsley and serve.

Lonza is a cured pork loin that is similar to prosciutto in taste and texture, yet easier to slice, thanks to its more uniform shape. You can find this delicious Italian specialty at Italian gourmet shops.

PROSCIUTTO AND MOZZARELLA TEA SANDWICH

(Panino con Prosciutto e Mozzarella)

Serves 4–6 people

6–8 fresh bakery dinner rolls

12–16 slices prosciutto (2 slices per sandwich)

½ pound fresh Mozzarella, sliced

Olive oil

Pinch of salt

¼ cup chopped fresh parsley

Slice rolls. Roll prosciutto and place two rolls in each sandwich. Layer with a slice of Mozzarella. Drizzle with a little olive oil and add salt. Top with parsley and serve.

BROCCOLI RABE FRITTATA TEA SANDWICH

(Panino con Frittata di Broccoli e Rape)

Serves 4–6 people

1 bunch fresh broccoli rabe

½ cup olive oil

3 garlic cloves, chopped

1 medium Spanish onion, chopped

¼ cup finely chopped fresh parsley

Pinch of salt and black pepper

6 large eggs

¼ cup freshly grated Pecorino Romano cheese

¼ cup whole milk

6–8 fresh bakery dinner rolls

1. Bring a medium saucepan of water to a boil. Add the broccoli rabe and boil for 10–15 minutes. Place ¼ cup olive oil and the garlic in a sauté pan and heat over medium heat. Remove broccoli rabe from the boiling water and sauté in the oil for 5 minutes. Remove from heat and set aside.

2. In a 10-inch frying pan, heat the remaining ¼ cup olive oil over medium-high heat. Add the onion and sauté for 2–3 minutes. Add the parsley, salt, and pepper, and sauté for an additional 2–3 minutes.

3. Beat the eggs, cheese, and milk in a glass bowl and slowly add to the onions, along with a pinch of salt. Increase the heat and use a spatula to keep the mixture from sticking to the pan. Lift the pan and tilt to allow the eggs to cook thoroughly. Once the egg becomes solid, the frittata is cooked. Remove from the heat and flip the frittata over onto a clean surface.

4. Using a biscuit cutter or a drinking glass (approximately the same size as your dinner rolls), cut circles out of the frittata. Slice the rolls and place a frittata patty into each sandwich. Top with a forkful of broccoli rabe and serve.

ITALIAN EGG SALAD TEA SANDWICH

(Panino con Insalata di Uova)

Serves 4–6 people

6 large eggs

½ cup grated celery

1 small onion, finely diced

½ cup finely diced green olives

1 teaspoon finely chopped fresh parsley

½ cup mayonnaise

1 teaspoon red chili pepper spread

Pinch of salt and black pepper

6–8 slices thinly sliced white sandwich bread

1. Fill a medium-sized saucepan three-fourths full with water and gently place eggs in the pan in their shells. Bring water to a boil and cook the eggs over medium heat for at least 10 minutes. Remove eggs from the water and rinse under cold water. Peel shells. Place hard-boiled eggs in a bowl, cover, and refrigerate for 20–30 minutes.

2. Chop eggs and place in a mixing bowl. Add the celery, onion, olives, parsley, mayonnaise, chili pepper spread, salt, and black pepper, and fold gently until thoroughly mixed.

3. Cut the crusts off the bread slices. Spoon desired amount of salad onto half of slices. Top with remaining bread slices. Cut each sandwich into four equal-sized squares.

CHICKEN SALAD TEA SANDWICH

(Panino con Insalata di Pollo)

Serves 4–6 people

For the chicken:

1 (5–6 pound) whole chicken

Salt, to taste

1 large whole onion, peeled

2 celery stalks, divided into thirds, including leaves

2 carrots, peeled and cut in half

For the salad:

1 celery stalk, cut into 1/8-inch slices

1/2 small onion, finely chopped

1 teaspoon fresh dill, chopped

1 tablespoon chopped fresh parsley

1 teaspoon red chili pepper spread

Pinch of salt and black pepper

Shredded chicken

1 cup mayonnaise

6–8 slices thinly sliced white sandwich bread or 6–8 fresh bakery dinner rolls

1. *Prepare the chicken:* Rinse the chicken inside and out under cold water and place in a large stockpot. Add about 6 quarts of water and a pinch of salt, until three-fourths of the chicken is covered with water. Bring water to a boil. As the chicken cooks, skim off the scum that rises to the surface. After the first hour, add onion, celery, and carrots, and simmer for an additional hour. Continue to skim off any scum that rises to the top. Remove the chicken from the pot and set aside in a bowl to cool. Once cool, remove breast and leg meat and transfer to a large mixing bowl. Shred the chicken with your hands. (Reserve the broth and chicken carcass for making soup.)

2. *Prepare the salad:* Add the celery, onion, dill, parsley, chili pepper spread, salt, and black pepper to the shredded chicken and mix thoroughly. Add the mayonnaise and blend thoroughly. Cut the crust off the bread slices or slice your rolls. Divide the chicken salad among half the bread slices and top with the remaining slices. Cut each sandwich into four equal-sized squares. If using rolls, divide the mixture among the sliced rolls.

"You will have two dishes when preparing the chicken. The broth can be used for one of my soups. This dish is one of many where my kids have taken my traditional recipe and given it a modern twist."

—ELISA

MINI PIZZAS

(Mini pizze)

Makes 2 ½ dozen mini pizzas

6 cups all-purpose flour,
plus more for dusting

2 envelopes active dry yeast

½ teaspoon salt

½ cup olive oil

2 cups vegetable oil

3 cups marinara sauce

4 cups freshly grated
Mozzarella cheese

1. In a small mixing bowl, place 1 cup of warm water, 1 cup of flour, and the yeast, and mix with a fork. Allow the mixture to sit in a warm place for 30–40 minutes.

2. After the yeast has rested, on a clean wooden or marble-like surface, make a mound with the remaining 5 cups of flour. Hollow out the center with a spoon. Add 2 cups of warm water, salt, and the yeast mixture to the well, and whisk with a fork, gradually adding the flour from the mound. Once you have incorporated all the flour, knead well until the dough has a uniform consistency.

3. Place the dough in an olive oil–greased bowl at least three times the size of the dough ball. Brush some olive oil on top of the dough, cover with a cloth, and allow it to rise in a warm place for 2–3 hours.

4. Cover a clean surface with some flour. Pinch off a piece of dough the size of a small orange and flatten it with a rolling pin, into a circle 3–4 inches in diameter. Continue to make more circles until you have used all the dough.

5. Heat vegetable oil in a large skillet over high heat until hot. Reduce the heat, then place a few dough circles into the skillet (avoid overcrowding the pan). Fry for 2–3 minutes, then flip and fry for an additional 2–3 minutes. The dough should turn a golden color. Remove the fried dough from the oil and dry it on a paper towel. Fry more mini pizzas in the same way.

6. Preheat the oven to 350°F.

7. Arrange the fried dough circles on ungreased baking sheets. Spread a teaspoon of marinara sauce on top of each circle, and then sprinkle cheese over the sauce. Bake for 10 minutes, until the cheese has melted. Remove from the oven, arrange on a serving platter, and serve.

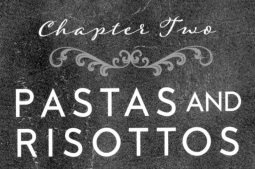

Chapter Two

PASTAS AND RISOTTOS

(PRIMI PIATTI)

EVOLUTION OF COOKING

My cooking style could best be described as traditional Italian that has been influenced by my upbringing in my hometown, Poggio Valle. I still cook many of the same dishes that I learned to make as a child, and I still follow the same principles that have always guided my meal preparation. Over the years, however, I have changed my recipes a great many times for numerous reasons. As nice as it is to be consistent, and as much as that helps to become efficient in the kitchen, a good cook also has to be adaptable.

In some cases, I have changed the way I prepare certain foods simply because I have other demands in my life. The way I make bread is a good example. Growing up, bread making was an arduous process that began with waking up at 2:00 or 3:00 in the early morning to work at the *casciona*, a large, freestanding, wooden breadbox with a hinged top. This traditional piece of "furniture" served as the epicenter of all bread-making activities. It had three internal compartments: On one side was old bread that would be soaked in warm water to produce yeast for future loaves; in the middle, proof of the new loaf would rest; and, on the other end, opposite the old bread, were the prepared loaves, ready for our family to eat.

On the bench top of the *casciona*, we would knead the mounds of dough that would become the bread. Because we were typically preparing more than one loaf at a time, the dough could weigh up to twenty-five pounds. Imagine how much labor and hard work it takes to knead and turn such a heavy portion of dough into sizes appropriate for baking!

My bread-making operation today is a much simpler process. While I make bread on special occasions, I admit that I occasionally go to the local bakery to select a loaf of bread to have with dinner. In either case, we do not eat bread with every meal, as we used to as children, or as they still do in Italy. So the frequency and scale of my bread making has changed dramatically. Also, I can now shop for ingredients at the store. We no longer have to haul the grain we grew in our village to the mill to process the flour, nor do we have to reuse old loaves of bread because of a scarcity of yeast. In fact, because of the widespread availability of yeast, I can use a much larger portion of it to speed up the process.

My cooking has evolved, in large part, because of the abundance of ingredients in America, and the fact that so many different kinds of foods are so readily available here, compared to where I grew up. I remember sitting down to dinner with my brother Joe when I first came to America. There were four of us at the table, and my sister-in-law, Pierina, brought out two whole chickens for us to dine on. I could not believe this, as it was rare back in our homeland that we could have chicken for dinner, much less two in the same meal.

I would soon learn that Americans have a very different outlook on food, especially when it comes to what is acceptable in terms of waste. Many people associate chicken cutlets with Italian cooking, but so much meat is wasted in preparing this recipe that it is a luxury in traditional Italian fare. Nevertheless, my family and I now regularly enjoy chicken cutlets, and, in many cases, they are prepared as a complement to the main dish.

And now, because I can go the supermarket and pick out fruits and vegetables and other items, I am not necessarily restricted to cooking what is in season. Growing up, meals consisted of what was available from the farm. In the winter, we ate a lot of pasta, prepared only with the tomato sauce we had jarred during the preceding summer; there were no fresh vegetables to add. We would also make sausage during the winter, curing and drying meats for dishes that would be made with them through the rest of the year. Come springtime, our meals would include cabbage and cauliflower, both hearty vegetables that ripened early in the season. By summer, vegetables were more abundant, and suddenly frittatas and vegetable-based dishes would predominate. Interestingly, because of the heat, and because our family would build up a greater appetite working the land in the warmer weather, we would eat four times a day, rather than three, as in other seasons.

Once in America, our menus became less seasonally oriented, and more often were inspired by our desires. Our family ate lots of pasta (mostly the store-bought variety), and on Fridays we ate fish and pizza to avoid eating meat. But on Saturday nights, we often cooked up steaks served with white rice and peas. This was, and still is, a fairly typical meal for most Americans, whereas steak was considered a luxury dish in Italy, and, even today, is rarely served during a family meal.

Changing tastes, changing times, changing circumstances—these are only a few factors over the years have that have influenced how I prepare meals. For example, because I worked as a professional cook for the residents of Divine Providence Village in Springfield, Pennsylvania, I was inspired to try new things in the kitchen at home. My dear Francesco would get so frustrated. "Why do you have to change?" he would ask. I could have easily become upset over this, feeling that he was telling me what to do. But looking at this another way, it was a compliment. After all, he liked the way I prepared food, so why should I ever change what he liked?

I loved my Francesco, but sometimes it is necessary to adjust the way a meal is prepared. I now have a Jewish granddaughter-in-law who does not eat pork and a granddaughter-in-law who is a vegetarian—facts that have forced me to modify my recipes at times. What these experiences have taught me is that while it is certainly nice to have traditions upon which to rely, it is also essential to stay receptive to new influences. If I were to suggest anything to the home cook, it would be to establish a style for yourself, a basis for thinking about ingredients, but to also be ready to vary the way you do things. This does not mean that one has to abandon one's foundation; instead, once the home cook has a firm grasp of how to prepare foods and what to do with them, it is rather easy to adjust for the loved ones gathered around your table.

PASTA FAGIOLI

Serves 6 people

Ingredients

1 (16-ounce) bag dried red kidney beans

1 ham bone

2 cups chopped celery

3 cups chopped onions

2 cups chopped carrots

1 cup chopped fresh parsley

½ cup olive oil

1 (28-ounce) can chopped tomatoes

1 pound fresh spaghetti, cut into 1-inch lengths, or dry orecchiette pasta (see Note)

Freshly grated Parmesan cheese, for garnish

Directions

1. Place beans in a bath of cold water for 6–8 hours prior to preparing the dish.

2. Drain soaked beans and place in a stockpot with the ham bone and 12 cups of water, bring to a boil, and boil for 15 minutes. Drain the beans, then add them back to the pan with the celery, 2 cups of the onions, the carrots, and the parsley. Add enough fresh hot water to cover all ingredients by 2 inches. Bring the beans and vegetables to a boil, then simmer for 1 hour, continuously adding more fresh hot water if needed to keep the water level 2 inches above all ingredients.

3. Meanwhile, add the remaining cup of onions and the oil to a sauté pan and sauté onions over low heat for a few minutes. Add the tomatoes and continue to sauté for 20–25 minutes more. Remove pan from the heat and set aside.

4. When the beans and vegetables have cooked for 1 hour, add the onions and tomatoes and keep warm.

5. Bring a separate stockpot with water to a boil and cook your pasta al dente. Drain pasta well and add to the bean-and-vegetable mixture. Transfer to a serving bowl and serve with Parmesan cheese.

NOTE

If you have the time to make homemade pasta, fresh mezzaluna or tagliolini pasta make a very nice presentation.

WALNUT AND RICOTTA RAVIOLI

(Ravioli di Ricotta e Noci)

Serves 6–8 people

Ingredients

9 jumbo eggs

3 pounds Ricotta cheese, drained

2 cups freshly grated Parmesan or Pecorino Romano cheese, plus more for garnish

1½ cups finely crushed walnuts, plus more for garnish

¼ cup finely chopped fresh parsley, plus more for garnish

Pinch of salt and black pepper

3½ cups all-purpose flour, plus more for dusting

Olive oil

1¼ cups butter, salted

8–10 fresh sage leaves

NOTE

I prefer to prepare my dough by hand, but you may choose to use an electric stand mixer with a dough hook.

Directions

1. In a glass bowl, beat 3 eggs, then add the Ricotta cheese, 1½ cups of the grated Parmesan or Pecorino Romano cheese, 1 cup of the walnuts, the parsley, and a pinch of salt and pepper. Mix thoroughly. Cover the mixture with plastic wrap and refrigerate until ready to use.

2. Mound the flour in the center of a clean large wooden board or flat work surface. Make a well in the center of the flour and add the remaining 6 eggs. Using a fork, beat the eggs together, then begin to incorporate the flour, starting with the inner rim of the well. As you expand the well, keep pushing the flour up to retain the well shape. When half of the flour is incorporated, the dough will begin to come together. Start kneading the dough, using primarily the palms of your hands. Once the dough is a cohesive shape, set the dough aside, scraping up and discarding any dried bits of dough.

3. Continue kneading the dough for 10 minutes, dusting your board or work surface with additional flour as necessary. The dough should be elastic and a little sticky. Place the dough in a bowl, spread olive oil around the dough mass, and cover. Allow to rest for 30 minutes at room temperature before proceeding.

4. Cut the dough into four equal-sized pieces. Cover them with a clean kitchen towel and keep covered when you are not handling the dough to keep it from drying out. Working with one piece of dough at a time, dust your work surface and dough with a little flour and press dough into a 5–6-thick rectangle. Roll through the widest setting on the pasta machine. Fold the rectangle of dough in half, and roll through again. Repeat the rolling and folding process a few more times, to knead and smooth the dough. Return dough to the covering cloth and repeat with the remaining dough pieces.

5. Switch to the next available setting on the machine. Roll a dough strip through the machine with the short end first. Repeat with the remaining dough strips. Continue this process through the narrower settings, now rolling only once through each setting, until you get to the next-to-last setting and the dough strips are about as wide as the machine (6 inches). Your final dough strips should be paper-thin, about ⅛ inch thick. Dust the sheets of dough with flour as needed.

6. Bring a large stockpot of water to a boil.

7. Working with one dough strip at a time, fill and cut the ravioli: Spread out the strip of pasta dough on a clean work surface dusted with flour. Starting 3 inches from one end, drop 1 tablespoon of filling in the center of the dough, and continue to drop filling every 3 inches. Fold over the pasta dough and press down on the ends where the pasta dough meets with your fingers. Using a wheel cutter, cut ravioli into moon shapes with a Ricotta mound centered on each cut. Fill and cut the remaining strips in the same way. Drop 4–6 ravioli at a time into the boiling water (do not crowd the stockpot) and boil for 5–7 minutes. Scoop out the ravioli with a slotted spoon and arrange on a serving platter. Cook the remaining ravioli in the same way.

8. While the ravioli is cooking, melt the butter in a large sauté pan over medium heat. Add the sage leaves, the remaining ½ cup crushed walnuts and the remaining ½ cup grated cheese, and sauté for 4–5 minutes. Pour your sauce over the cooked ravioli. Garnish with more walnuts, cheese, and parsley and serve.

ORECCHIETTE WITH ASPARAGUS AND SAFFRON

(Orecchiette con Asparagi e Zafferano)

Serves 4–6 people

Ingredients

2 garlic cloves, chopped

¼ cup olive oil

¼ cup salted butter

2 cups fresh asparagus, cut into
2-inch pieces

½ cup grated fresh carrots

¼ cup chopped fresh basil

Pinch of salt

1 tablespoon saffron

1 pound dry orecchiette pasta, or
prepare your own fresh egg pasta

¼ cup freshly grated Parmesan or
Pecorino Romano cheese

Directions

1. In a large sauté pan, sauté the garlic in olive oil over medium heat. Add the butter, asparagus, carrots, basil, and salt, and continue to sauté until the asparagus is tender. In a small saucepan, bring 2 cups of water and the saffron to a simmer (5–7 minutes).

2. While the asparagus is cooking, bring a large stockpot of water to a boil and cook pasta according to package instructions. Drain pasta and place in a serving bowl. Top pasta with the asparagus mixture and pour the saffron water over the pasta. Add the cheese, toss thoroughly, and serve.

"Years ago, we were visiting our hometown, and Francesco and I went on a early morning walk with our grandchildren. Along the way, Sebastian asked us why an old man we encountered was picking weeds on the side of the road. Francesco explained to him that he wasn't picking weeds, but rather wild asparagus growing on the side of the road. We told the children that searching along the road or in the mountains for asparagus, truffles, and herbs that could be used in the kitchen was usually how many older members of the town contributed food to their families or bartered for other goods. Francesco loved sharing stories of his childhood and the mountains surrounding his hometown, and Sebastian, especially, always showed great interest in hearing about our shared heritage. In 2015, we were once again visiting, but this time Francesco was no longer with us. I took that same walk along the same road with my grandchildren, and I reminded them of our previous walk years before. Shortly afterwards, we spotted some asparagus on the side of the road. We picked it and enjoyed this dish for lunch that day."

—ELISA

SAUSAGE PAELLA

(Paella di Salsiccia)

Serves 4–6 people

Ingredients

½ cup olive oil

2 garlic cloves, minced

2 Spanish onions, chopped

3–4 red and green bell peppers, chopped

3 cups sausage, removed from casing

1 cup chopped pancetta

1 teaspoon saffron

2 cups Arborio rice

½ cup dry white wine, plus more if necessary

2 cups fresh or canned crushed tomatoes

1 bay leaf

Pinch of salt and black pepper

Directions

1. In a large sauté pan with a lid, heat the olive oil and garlic over medium heat. Add the onions and bell peppers and sauté for 5 minutes. Add the sausage and pancetta and sauté for 10 minutes more.

2. In a small bowl, mix together 1 cup of water and the saffron.

3. When the sausage has cooked for 10 minutes, add the rice, saffron water, wine, tomatoes, and bay leaf. Mix thoroughly for 2–3 minutes, and bring to a boil. Add a pinch of salt and pepper, reduce the heat, and simmer, covered, stirring occasionally, until all the liquid is absorbed and the rice is cooked to taste. If the liquid is absorbed before the rice is cooked, add additional wine and water and continue to cook. Remove pan from the heat. Transfer paella to a serving plate and serve.

"Although paella is traditionally considered a Spanish dish, we know through history that as one culture conquered or traded with another, culinary lines were crossed. Paella is most commonly known in eastern Spain, primarily along the coast, and the Spaniards often traded with the west coast of Italy. Paella is very similar to risotto, with the addition of saffron. Today, some of the best paella in Europe can be found in Venezia."

—ELISA

NOTE
*You can create a lobster
bisque by adding additional
heavy cream and
mini raviolis.*

PENNE WITH LOBSTER

(Penne all'Aragosta)

Ingredients

¼ cup butter, salted

2 pounds cooked lobster meat (fresh or thawed frozen), chopped

¼ cup olive oil

1 cooked lobster tail
(fresh or thawed frozen)

4 garlic cloves, minced

2 Spanish onions, chopped

¼ cup chopped fresh parsley,
plus more for garnish

2 teaspoons red chili peppers,
minced, plus more for garnish

2 whole bay leaves

1 cup seafood or chicken stock

½ cup dry white wine

Salt and black pepper, to taste

2 (28-ounce) cans crushed
tomatoes

1 pound penne dry pasta

½ cup heavy cream

Freshly grated Parmesan and
Pecorino Romano cheese,
for garnish

Directions

1. Bring a large pot of water to a boil for pasta.

2. Heat the butter in a large sauté pan over medium heat, then add 2 pounds chopped lobster meat (not the lobster tail) and sauté for 2–3 minutes. Transfer lobster and any juices to a bowl and set aside.

3. Place olive oil in the same pan and heat over medium heat. Add the lobster tail, garlic, onions, parsley, chili peppers, and bay leaves, and sauté for 5–7 minutes. Add the reserved lobster meat, stock, and wine, bring to a rapid simmer, and cook for about 5 minutes. Add a pinch of salt and black pepper to taste. Reduce heat to low, then add crushed tomatoes and simmer for 25–30 minutes.

4. Meanwhile, cook penne until al dente according to the package instructions.

5. When the lobster mixture has simmered for 25–30 minutes, add the heavy cream and mix thoroughly. Reduce heat to the lowest setting and add salt to taste.

6. Drain the pasta and place it in a serving bowl. Pour the lobster mixture over the pasta and toss thoroughly. Garnish with parsley, cheese, and chili peppers, and serve.

"If you are using live whole lobsters, boil the lobsters, remove all the meat from the cavity and claws, and save the tail. If you are using frozen lobster meat, be sure to thaw it out in a strainer to drain any excess water, and wait to add your lobster until you add your crushed tomatoes."

—ELISA

GNOCCHI WITH TRUFFLES

(Gnocchi ai Tartufi)

Serves 4–6 people

Ingredients

5 pounds russet potatoes

4 cups all-purpose flour, plus more for dusting

4 large eggs

¼ cup olive oil

Salt and black pepper

2 cups butter, salted

½ cup olive oil

1 garlic clove, minced

4–5 fresh sage leaves

1–2 tablespoons fresh grated truffles, to taste

Directions

1. Place the potatoes in a large stockpot and fill the pot about three-fourths full with water. Place pot over medium-high heat and boil potatoes until tender, about 30 minutes. Drain and let the potatoes cool. Once they are cool enough to handle, peel them.

2. Pass potatoes through a potato ricer or grate them on the large holes of a box grater. (This should produce about 8 cups of grated potatoes.) On a wooden or marble-like work surface, make a mound with flour and spoon out a well in the middle. Add the eggs to the well and beat the eggs with a fork. Mix in the potatoes, oil, and 1 tablespoon salt, and begin to fold in the flour. Once enough flour has been added to absorb the eggs, fold in the rest of the flour, using your hands to form a dough. If the mixture is too dry, add a little water. The dough should bounce back under slight pressure.

3. Lightly flour your work surface, and cut the dough into 6 equal-sized pieces. Roll each piece into a rope about ½ inch in diameter, then cut diagonally into 1-inch-long pieces. Lightly flour the gnocchi as you cut them. Place cut gnocchi on floured baking sheets.

4. Bring a large pot of water to a boil and add a pinch of salt.

5. *Meanwhile, prepare your sauce:* In a large sauté pan, melt the butter over medium heat. Add the olive oil, garlic, and sage leaves, and sauté for 4–5 minutes.

6. Drop the gnocchi into the boiling water and cook. When they rise to the surface, wait 1 minute, then remove with a skimmer and drain thoroughly. Add the gnocchi to the sauce and toss to combine. Add a pinch of salt and pepper and transfer to a serving platter. Grate the fresh truffles over the gnocchi and serve.

TUMBLING OVER TRUFFLES

Truffles are a gourmet delicacy, one of the most expensive and coveted in the world. Growing up, we were fortunate to find truffles easily while out in the fields, or on our walks to the nearby city of Teramo. Accompanied by our family dogs, who were attracted to the aroma, they would lead us to these underground treasures. Although many people have tried to farm truffles, they are difficult to cultivate.

Many truffles are still harvested today in the wild by truffle hunters who use dogs, and even pigs, that are trained to sniff them out. My nephews still practice this hunting hobby today, and every summer I try to participate in at least one truffle hunt. I retrace the same walking paths that I traveled over fifty years ago and find that they are still filled with these delightful additions to many pasta and risotto dishes. An estimated 80 percent of Italy's truffles are grown in Abruzzo.

—ELISA

SPINACH PASTA

(Pasta Agli Spinaci)

Ingredients

1 pound fresh spinach

Pinch of salt

3 ½ cups all-purpose flour,
plus more for dusting

6 jumbo eggs

Olive oil

Directions

1. Bring a medium saucepan filled with water to a boil. Add spinach and a pinch of salt to the boiling water and cook for 10–15 minutes. Drain and allow to cool. Once cool, chop finely and set aside.

2. Mound the flour in the center of a clean, large, wooden or marble-like work surface. Make a well in the center of the flour and add the eggs. Using a fork, beat the eggs together. Add the spinach to the well and begin to incorporate the flour, starting with the inner rim of the well. As the well expands, keep pushing the flour up to retain the well shape. (Do not worry if it looks messy.)

3. When half of the flour is incorporated, the dough will begin to come together. Start kneading the dough, using primarily the palms of your hands. Once the dough is a cohesive shape, set the dough aside, scraping up and discarding any dried bits of dough. Continue kneading for 10 minutes, dusting the board with additional flour, as necessary.

The dough should be elastic and a little sticky. Place the dough in a bowl, spread olive oil around the dough, and cover with a kitchen towel. Allow the dough to rest for 30 minutes at room temperature before proceeding.

4. Cut the dough into four equal-sized pieces. Cover them with a clean kitchen towel and keep them covered when you are not handling them to prevent them from drying out. Working with one piece of dough at a time, dust your work surface and dough with a little flour and press the dough into a 5 to 6-inch-thick rectangle. Roll through the widest setting on the pasta machine. Fold the rectangle of dough in half, and roll it through again. Repeat the rolling and folding process a few more times, to knead and smooth the dough. Return the dough to the covering cloth and repeat with the remaining dough pieces.

5. Switch to the next available setting on the machine. Roll a dough strip through the machine with the short end first. Repeat with the remaining dough strips. Continue this process through the narrower settings, now rolling only once through each setting, until you get to the next-to-last setting and the dough strips are about as wide as the machine (6 inches).

6. *Cut the strips into the desired shape:* For tagliatelle, starting with a long side, roll up the strips tightly, then, using a sharp knife, cut the roll into ½-inch-wide slices. For spaghetti or linguine, use the appropriate setting on your pasta machine.

7. Serve the pasta with a cream or butter-based sauce (see chapter 5, "Sauces, Condiments, and Preserves" [*Salse, Condimenti e Conserve*], page 219).

VEGETABLE TIMBALLO

(Timballo di Verdure)

Ingredients

For the crêpes:

10 jumbo eggs

2½ cups all-purpose flour

1 cup olive oil

For the filling:

¼ cup olive oil

1 large Spanish onion, chopped

2 garlic cloves, chopped

2 zucchini, chopped

1 eggplant, peeled and chopped

1½ cups peas

2 celery stalks, thinly sliced

3 carrots, peeled and thinly sliced

1 10-ounce carton frozen leaf spinach, drained and chopped

Pinch of salt and fresh black pepper

2 eggs

½ cup whole milk

(continues on next page)

Directions

1. *Prepare the crêpes:* Beat the eggs at a low speed in the bowl of an electric stand mixer, fitted with a beater attachment, then gradually sift in the flour. Continue to beat at a very low speed for 5–10 minutes while gradually adding 3½ cups of water. Continue to beat until the batter is very smooth, with no visible lumps (approximately 5 minutes).

2. Heat an 8- or 10-inch nonstick pan over low heat. (You must use a nonstick pan to keep the crêpes from burning and sticking to the pan. An 8-inch pan yields 40–45 crêpes; a 10-inch pan yields 25–30 crêpes.) Put the olive oil in a small bowl. Dip a paper towel into the olive oil and grease the pan; you will need to repeat the greasing of the pan after every 3 or 4 crêpes. Using a ladle, spread batter lightly to cover the entire surface of the pan. Allow the crêpe to cook for 2–3 minutes, then remove it with a fork and transfer it to a paper towel–covered work surface. Add some water to the batter if it becomes too thick and does not run easily over the pan. Line the finished crêpes on paper towels (do not stack them) until ready to use

3. Preheat the oven to 350°F.

4. *Prepare the filling:* In a medium sauté pan, heat the olive oil over medium heat and sauté the onions and garlic until the onions are soft. Add the zucchini, eggplant, peas, celery, carrots, spinach, salt, and pepper, and continue to sauté them until all vegetables are tender. Drain the oil and set the vegetables aside. In a separate bowl, beat the eggs and milk.

5. *Assemble the timballo:* Add a layer of crêpes to the bottom of a greased 13 x 9 x 2-inch glass casserole pan, overlapping them slightly. Brush crêpes with the egg mixture. Layer with some vegetables, and top with some Mozzarella and Parmesan cheese.

2 pounds fresh
Mozzarella
cheese, shredded

½ cup freshly grated
Parmesan cheese

6 cups vegetable stock

8 tablespoons salted butter,
cut into small cubes

6. Pour half a ladleful of vegetable broth over the crêpes and sprinkle with a few cubes (about 1 tablespoon) of butter. Continue layering with the remaining ingredients in the same way. (The top layer should have a healthy portion of broth and grated cheese.) Cover with parchment paper and then with foil and bake for 60–90 minutes, or until most of the liquid is evaporated. Remove from the oven and allow to sit for 20 minutes before serving.

NOTE

Any extra crêpes can be frozen and used on another occasion for soup.

TAGLIATELLE WITH BLACK TRUFFLE AND MUSHROOM CREAM SAUCE

(Tagliatelle al Tartufo Nero e Crema di Funghi)

Serves 4–6 people

Ingredients

3 ½ cups all-purpose flour, plus more for dusting

6 jumbo eggs

Olive oil

½ cup (8 tablespoons) butter, salted

½ pound Porcini mushrooms, chopped

1 cup green peas

3 garlic cloves, chopped

Pinch of salt and black pepper

1 cup dry white wine

¼ cup chopped fresh parsley

4 cups heavy cream

3 tablespoons freshly grated black truffles

½ cup freshly grated Parmesan and Pecorino Romano cheese

Directions

1. Mound the flour in the center of a clean, large, wooden or marble-like work surface. Make a well in the center of the flour and add the eggs. Using a fork, beat the eggs together. Begin to incorporate the flour, starting with the inner rim of the well. As the well expands, keep pushing the flour up to retain the well shape. (Do not worry if it looks messy.)

2. When half the flour is incorporated, the dough will begin to come together. Start kneading the dough, using primarily the palms of your hands. Once the dough is a cohesive shape, set the dough aside, scraping up and discarding any dried bits of dough. Continue kneading for 10 minutes, dusting the board or work surface with additional flour as necessary. The dough should be elastic and a little sticky. Place dough in a bowl, spread olive oil all over the dough mass, and cover. Allow the dough to rest for 30 minutes at room temperature before proceeding.

3. Cut the dough into four equal-sized pieces. Cover them with a clean kitchen towel and keep them covered when you are not handling them to prevent them from drying out. Working with one piece of dough at a time, dust your work surface and dough with a little flour and press the dough into a rectangle. Roll through the widest setting on the pasta machine. Fold the rectangle of dough in half, and roll it through again. Repeat the rolling and folding process a few more times, to knead and smooth the dough. Return the dough to the covering cloth and repeat with the remaining dough pieces.

4. Switch to the next available setting on the machine. Roll a dough strip through the machine with the short end first. Repeat with the remaining dough strips. Continue this process through the narrower settings, now rolling only once through each setting, until you get to the next-to-last setting and the dough strips are about as wide as the machine (6 inches). Dust the sheets of dough with flour as needed.

5. Starting with a long side, roll up each of the fresh egg pasta strips tightly. Using a sharp knife, slice the roll into ½-inch-wide slices.

6. Bring to a boil a large stockpot of water and a pinch of salt.

7. Meanwhile, *prepare the sauce:* Melt the butter in a large sauté pan over medium-high heat. Add the mushrooms, peas, garlic, salt, and pepper, and sauté for 6–8 minutes. Add the wine and parsley, and continue to sauté for 5 minutes. Reduce the heat, then add the heavy cream and half the truffles, and simmer, stirring occasionally, for 10 minutes, or until thickened.

8. Drop the pasta into the boiling water and cook for 3–4 minutes. Remove from the heat and drain well. Add the pasta to the sauce, add the cheese, and toss thoroughly. Transfer to a serving bowl and garnish with the remaining truffles.

NOTE
*If you do not have the time to prepare fresh pasta, you can use a
1-pound box of tagliatelle dry pasta instead.*

SAUSAGE AND PANCETTA RIGATONI WITH TOMATO CREAM SAUCE

(Rigatoni al Sugo con Salsiccia e Pancetta)

Serves 4–6 people

Ingredients

¼ cup olive oil

2 garlic cloves, minced

1 cup diced red bell peppers or red roasting peppers

1 cup diced white onions

1½ pounds Italian sausage, crumbled

8 ounces pancetta, cubed

Salt and black pepper, to taste

2 (28-ounce) cans crushed tomatoes

¼ cup chopped fresh basil

¼ cup chopped fresh oregano

¼ cup chopped fresh parsley

2 teaspoons crushed hot red pepper flakes, or jarred red peppers, plus more for garnish

1 pound rigatoni or mezzi rigatoni dry pasta

1 pint heavy cream

1 cup freshly grated Parmesan cheese, plus more for garnish

½ cup freshly grated Pecorino Romano cheese, plus more for garnish

Directions

1. In a large sauté pan, heat the olive oil and garlic over medium heat for 2–3 minutes. Add the red bell peppers and onions, and sauté for 5–7 minutes, until onions begin to soften. Add the sausage, pancetta, and salt and black pepper to taste, and sauté until sausage is fully cooked.

2. Meanwhile, bring to a boil a large stockpot of water and a pinch of salt.

3. When the sausage is cooked, drain the oil and fat from the sauté pan, add the crushed tomatoes, basil, oregano, parsley, and red pepper flakes, and continue to cook over medium heat until the mixture begins to boil.

4. Drop the rigatoni into the boiling water and cook al dente according to package instructions.

5. When the tomato mixture begins to boil, reduce the heat, add the heavy cream and cheeses to the sausage mixture, and mix thoroughly. Drain the pasta and transfer to a serving bowl. Pour the sauce over the pasta and toss. Garnish with additional cheese and red pepper flakes to taste and serve immediately.

LENTIL STEW

(Zuppa di Lenticchie)

Serves 4–6 people

Ingredients

¼ cup olive oil

3 cloves garlic, minced

1 medium onion, finely chopped

1 cup finely chopped carrots

1 cup finely chopped celery

1½ cups canned lentils
(see Note below)

1½ cups peeled and cubed potatoes

3 bay leaves

2 (28-ounce) cans crushed
tomatoes with basil

¼ cup chopped fresh parsley,
plus more for serving

½ pound dry orecchiette pasta

Salt, to taste

¼ cup freshly grated Pecorino
Romano cheese, for garnish

Directions

1. Heat the olive oil, garlic, and onion in a large saucepan with a lid over medium heat for 2–3 minutes, then add the carrots and celery, and sauté for 5 minutes. Add 6 cups of water, the lentils, potatoes, and bay leaves, and simmer for 20 minutes. Add the crushed tomatoes and parsley. Bring the vegetable mixture to a boil, then reduce the heat and simmer, covered, for 20 minutes more. Add an additional cup of water and the orecchiette and continue to simmer until the pasta is cooked. Add salt to taste.

2. Remove from the heat and place in bowls. Garnish with Pecorino Romano cheese and parsley, and serve.

NOTE

*If you prefer to use dried lentils, boil them for
15–20 minutes and drain them.*

"This is a wonderful vegetarian meal on a cold winter day. The first winter that I spent in San Massimo with Francesco and his family I was introduced to this dish, which was served quite often throughout the cold winter months."

—ELISA

LINGUINE WITH TOMATOES AND ARTICHOKES

(Linguine al Sugo con Carciofi)

Ingredients

¼ cup olive oil

4 garlic cloves, whole

1 large Spanish onion, chopped

2 (28-ounce) cans crushed tomatoes

¼ cup chopped fresh basil

¼ cup chopped fresh parsley

Pinch of salt

2 cups marinated artichoke hearts, drained

1 pound dry linguine pasta or 1 pound fresh pasta

1 cup freshly grated Parmesan cheese

1 cup freshly grated Pecorino Romano cheese

Directions

1. Heat the olive oil, garlic, and onion in a large saucepan over medium heat for 2–3 minutes. Add the tomatoes, basil, parsley, and salt, and bring to a boil. Reduce the heat, add 1 cup of water and the marinated artichokes, and simmer the sauce for 1 hour, stirring occasionally, and adding more water if needed.

2. Bring to a boil a large stockpot of water and a pinch of salt. Drop the linguine into the boiling water and cook al dente according to package instructions. Drain the pasta, reserving 1 cup of cooking water, and place the pasta in a large serving bowl. Add the cup of cooking water and mix thoroughly. Ladle the sauce over the pasta and toss. Add the Parmesan and Pecorino Romano cheeses and toss thoroughly. Serve immediately.

SPAGHETTI WITH LAMB AND SAFFRON

(Spaghetti con Agnello e Zafferano)

Serves 4–6 people

Ingredients

For the pasta:

3 ½ cups all-purpose flour,
plus more for dusting

6 eggs

Pinch of salt

For the sauce:

¼ cup olive oil

1 large Spanish onion

3 garlic cloves, chopped

2 cups chicken or beef stock

¼ teaspoon saffron

1 ½ pounds lamb, cut into cubes
(see Notes below)

2 sprigs rosemary

Pinch of salt and black pepper

2 (28-ounce) cans crushed
tomatoes with basil

2 bay leaves

½ cup freshly grated Pecorino
Romano cheese, for garnish

Directions

1. *Prepare the pasta:* Create a mound of flour on a clean surface and scoop out a hole in the center. Add the eggs to the center with a pinch of salt and beat the eggs into the flour with a fork until the two have formed a solid mixture. Knead into a satiny ball of dough. Flatten the dough to about ½ inch thick with a rolling pin dusted with flour. Using your chitarra, pass sheets of flattened dough through the wooden frame; if you do not have one, use a more modern pasta machine.

2. *Prepare the sauce:* In a large sauté pan with a lid, heat the oil over medium heat, then add the onions and garlic, and sauté for 10–12 minutes, until onions are soft and translucent.

3. Meanwhile, in a small saucepan, heat the stock and saffron for 5–7 minutes.

4. When the onions are soft, add the lamb to the sauté pan with rosemary and a pinch of salt and pepper, and sauté for 4–5 minutes. Add the warm stock, reduce the heat, and simmer, covered, for 10 minutes. Add the tomatoes and bay leaves and continue to simmer for 20 minutes.

5. Bring a large stockpot of water to a boil and cook the fresh pasta until al dente, about 3–4 minutes. Drain pasta and place in a serving bowl. Ladle the lamb sauce over the pasta and toss thoroughly. Garnish with the Pecorino Romano cheese and serve.

NOTES

If you do not have time to make fresh pasta, you can substitute 1 pound of dry spaghetti and cook until al dente according to package instructions. Also, when choosing the lamb for this dish, meat on the bone is always best because it has a bit of fat around the bone that adds flavor to the dish, but you can use stewing meat, too.

"Saffron grows throughout the mountainous plateaus of Abruzzo and is considered one of the finest saffrons in the world. It is still the tradition for many families in our region to pick the plants by hand, then remove the pistils and dry them in their homes. Each flower usually has three pistils, and it takes more than fourteen thousand pistils to make one ounce of saffron. This can explain why the cost of saffron is so high in comparison to other herbs and spices. However, the flavor and aroma of saffron are so strong, you do not need much of it for your dish."

—FRANK

FRANCESCO'S LINGUINE

(Linguine de Francesco)

Serves 4–6 people

Ingredients

1 cup olive oil

2 large Spanish onions, chopped

½ pound Italian sausage, chopped (optional)

1 pound dry linguine pasta

2 large fresh ripe tomatoes, chopped

4 basil leaves, chopped, plus more for garnish

2½ cups whole milk

Salt and red pepper, to taste

½ cup freshly grated Pecorino Romano cheese, for garnish

Directions

1. In a large sauté pan or wok, heat the olive oil over low heat. Add the onions and sauté for 10 minutes. Add the sausage and continue to sauté for 20 minutes more.

2. Meanwhile, bring to a boil a large stockpot of water and a pinch of salt.

3. After the sausage and onion mixture has cooked for 20 minutes, drop the linguine into the boiling water and cook for about 4–5 minutes, half the recommend cooking time on the package.

4. While the pasta is cooking, add the tomatoes and half the basil to the onions and sausage. Drain the parcooked pasta and add to the sauce. Slowly pour in the milk, then add the remaining basil, a pinch of salt, and red pepper to taste. Toss the pasta through the sauce for about 5–7 minutes, until pasta is al dente.

5. Transfer to a serving bowl and garnish with the cheese, the remaining basil, and the red pepper. Serve immediately.

"This is a dish that my Francesco would prepare for me often. Toward the end of his life, he took a liking to cooking, and since he was usually home before I returned from work, he would surprise me with dinner prepared. This was one of the dishes he was most proud of. I never made this dish without him, and never spoke of it until we started to write this book. When I finally prepared the dish for my family, everyone agreed that it was something special and needed to be included. So when you make this dish, raise your wineglass and toast my husband."

—ELISA

ST. JOSEPH'S DAY PASTA

(Pappardelle di San Giuseppe)

Serves 4–6 people

Ingredients

For the pasta:

3 ½ cups all-purpose flour, plus more for dusting

6 jumbo eggs

Olive oil

For the sauce:

Pinch of salt

12 anchovy fillets (optional) (see Note on page 81)

1½ cups olive oil

4 garlic cloves, chopped

¼ cup chopped fresh parsley

1 cup Italian breadcrumbs, plus more for garnish

1 cup freshly grated Pecorino Romano cheese, plus more for garnish

Directions

1. *Prepare the pasta:* Mound the flour in the center of a clean, large wooden or marble-like work surface. Make a well in the center of the flour and add the eggs. Using a fork, beat eggs together, then begin to incorporate the flour, starting with the inner rim of the well. As you expand the well, keep pushing the flour up to retain the well shape. (Do not worry if it looks messy.)

2. When half the flour is incorporated, the dough will begin to come together. Start kneading the dough, using primarily the palms of your hands. Once the dough is a cohesive shape, set the dough aside, and scrape up and discard any dried bits of dough.

3. Continue kneading for 10 minutes, dusting the surface or the board with additional flour as necessary. The dough should be elastic and a little sticky. Put the dough in a bowl, spread olive oil around the dough mass, cover it, and allow it to rest for 30 minutes at room temperature before proceeding.

4. *Prepare the sauce:* Bring to a boil a large stockpot of water and a pinch of salt. Drain the anchovies well, and then chop them. Place the oil, garlic, and anchovies in a large sauté pan over medium heat and sauté for 4–5 minutes. Remove from heat and set aside.

5. When the dough has rested for 30 minutes, cut the dough into four equal-sized pieces. Cover them with a clean kitchen towel and keep them covered when you're not handling the dough to keep it from drying out. Working with one piece of dough at a time, dust your work surface and dough with a little flour and press the dough into a 5- to 6-inch-thick rectangle. Roll through the widest setting on the pasta machine. Fold the rectangle of dough in half, and roll it through again. Repeat the rolling and folding process a few more times, to knead and smooth the dough. Return the dough to the covering cloth and repeat with the remaining dough pieces.

6. Switch to the next available setting on the machine. Roll a dough strip through the machine with the short end first. Repeat with the remaining dough strips. Continue this process through the narrower settings, now rolling only once through each setting, until you get to the next-to-last setting and the dough strips are about as wide as the machine (6 inches). Dust the sheets of dough with flour as needed. Cut the dough strips into 3 x 1-inch rectangular strips with a knife or cutting wheel to form your pappardelle.

7. When the water in the stockpot is boiling, drop 3–4 strips of pappardelle into the boiling water and cook for 3–4 minutes. Remove pasta with a handheld strainer, arrange on kitchen towels to drain, and allow to cool. Cook the remaining pasta strips in the same way (reserve pasta cooking water).

8. Return the sauté pan to medium heat and add 1 cup of the pasta water to the anchovy sauce. Add the parsley, a pinch of salt, and the breadcrumbs, and blend thoroughly.

9. Place the cooked pappardelle in a serving bowl, a few at a time, while adding some of the sauce and the cheese. Continue layering the pasta, sauce, and cheese into the serving bowl until all the pasta is used. Garnish with additional breadcrumbs and cheese and serve.

NOTE

You can omit the anchovies or, if you'd like, use sautéed mushrooms instead.

SAFFRON PARMESAN RISOTTO

(Risotto di Zafferano e Parmigiano)

Serves 4–6 people

Ingredients

3–4 cups chicken stock

1 teaspoon saffron

¼ cup olive oil

1 large Spanish onion, chopped

2 cups Arborio rice

½ cup dry white wine

4 tablespoons butter, salted

¼ cup freshly grated Parmesan cheese, plus more for garnish

¼ cup freshly grated Pecorino Romano cheese, plus more for garnish

Directions

1. In a saucepan, heat the stock over medium-high heat and stir in the saffron. Keep the stock mixture warm as you prepare the risotto.

2. In a large sauté pan with a lid, heat the oil over medium-high heat for 2–3 minutes. Add the onion and sauté for 5 minutes. Reduce the heat, then add the rice and wine, mixing thoroughly. Add 2 ladlesful of stock and stir to combine. Continue to add more stock, one ladleful at a time, to keep the rice from drying out. Depending on the heat of your stove, the amount of stock needed will vary. The risotto is fully cooked when it's tender. Cooking time is about 20 minutes.

3. Remove pan from the heat. Add the butter and cheeses and fold thoroughly into the rice. Cover and allow to rest for 5 minutes before serving. Transfer to individual bowls, garnish with cheese, and serve.

BLACK TRUFFLE RISOTTO

(Risotto al Tartufo Nero)

Serves 4–6 people

4–6 cups vegetable stock

¼ cup olive oil

1 large Spanish onion, chopped

2 cups Arborio rice

1 cup dry white wine

Salt and black pepper, to taste

1 black truffle (about 3 ounces)

4 tablespoons salted butter

¼ cup freshly grated Parmesan cheese, plus more for garnish

Directions

1. In a saucepan, heat the stock over medium-high heat and keep warm as you prepare the risotto.

2. In a large sauté pan with a lid, heat the oil over medium-high heat for 2–3 minutes. Add the onion and sauté for 5 minutes. Reduce the heat, then add the rice and wine, and mix thoroughly. Add two ladlesful of stock and stir to combine. Continue to stir and add stock, one ladleful at a time, to keep the rice from drying out. Add salt and pepper to taste. Depending on the heat of your stove, the amount of stock needed will vary. The risotto is fully cooked when it's tender. Cooking time is about 20 minutes.

3. Remove pan from the heat. Shave the truffle very finely, using a razor blade or a mandolin slicer. Add the truffle shavings, butter, and cheese and fold thoroughly into the rice. Transfer to individual bowls, garnish with cheese, and serve.

PEA AND PANCETTA RISOTTO

(Risotto con Piselli e Pancetta)

Ingredients

6–8 cups chicken stock

¼ cup olive oil

2 cups diced pancetta

2 cups frozen peas, thawed

3 garlic cloves, minced

1 cup chopped Spanish onions

2 cups Arborio rice

1 cup dry white wine

Salt and black pepper, to taste

2 tablespoons butter, salted

½ cup freshly grated Parmesan or Pecorino Romano cheese, plus more for garnish

Directions

1. Heat the stock over medium-high heat and keep warm while preparing the risotto.

2. In a large sauté pan with a lid, heat the oil over medium-high heat for 2–3 minutes. Add the pancetta, peas, garlic, and onion, and sauté for 5–7 minutes. Reduce the heat, add the rice and wine, and mix thoroughly. Add two ladlesful of the stock and stir. Continue to stir and add stock, one ladleful at a time, to keep the rice from drying out. Add salt and pepper to taste. Depending on the heat of your stove, the amount of stock needed will vary. The risotto is fully cooked when it's tender. Cooking time is about 20 minutes.

3. Remove pan from the heat. Add the butter and cheese and fold thoroughly into the rice. Transfer to individual bowls, garnish with cheese, and serve.

CHICKEN RISOTTO

(Risotto di Pollo)

Serves 4–6 people

6–8 cups chicken stock

¼ cup olive oil

3 garlic cloves, chopped

2–3 chicken breasts, cubed

1 Spanish onion, chopped

1 green bell pepper, chopped

1 yellow bell pepper, chopped

2 cups chopped mushrooms
(see Note)

Pinch of salt and black pepper

2 cups Arborio rice

1 cup dry white wine

2 tablespoons butter, salted

½ cup freshly grated Parmesan
or Pecorino Romano cheese,
plus more for garnish

Directions

1. Heat the stock over medium-high heat and keep warm while preparing the risotto.

2. In a large sauté pan with a lid, heat the oil and garlic over medium-high heat for 2–3 minutes. Add the chicken, onion, bell peppers, and mushrooms, and sauté for 5–7 minutes. Add a pinch of salt and black pepper. Reduce the heat, then add the rice and wine and mix thoroughly. Add two ladlesful of stock and stir. Continue to stir and add stock, one ladleful at a time, to keep the rice from drying out. Add salt and pepper to taste. Depending on the heat of your stove, the amount of stock needed will vary. The risotto is fully cooked when it's tender. Cooking time is about 20 minutes.

3. Remove pan from the heat. Add the butter and cheese and fold thoroughly into the rice. Transfer to individual bowls, garnish with cheese, and serve.

NOTE
*Portobello mushrooms are particularly
delicious in this recipe!*

Chapter Three

SOUPS

(MINESTRE)

FESTAS AND STONE SOUP:
WHEN A COMMUNITY COMES TOGETHER

During the spring and summer months, and usually in conjunction with religious celebrations, many towns and villages throughout the Italian countryside host *festas*. These outdoor *festivals* are a community experience steeped in many traditions, mainly centered on the regional cuisine. But they serve an important social function, too. Because many are held in mountain towns, they are a perfect excuse for city dwellers to leave their congested urban milieu to spend time in the open air, eating, dancing, and sharing traditions. These festas are about families, friends, and strangers coming together, sharing what resources they have for the event. No one keeps score or measures what one brings over another.

It was at one of these *festas* many years ago that I met my first boyfriend, who was visiting from another village. I call him a boyfriend, but our relationship was more of a friendship. He lived very far away, and he courted me by traveling to our *festas* in order to spend time with me, and maybe steal a dance. I was young, but this was how relationships began. This particular relationship, however, was not to be. During one of our *festas*, another young man, my Francesco, rode into town on his motorcycle and stole my heart. The memories of those times stay with me. To this day, this festival remains very special to me, and I make certain to make the trip back to Italy to attend each year.

In Francesco's hometown of San Massimo, the *festa* lasts three days. Each day is truly an all-day event; in the morning, everyone gathers in the town square to share coffee and breakfast before starting to prepare for that evening's events. It is hard to describe in words the communal feeling of friends and strangers coming together, bringing their own talents and gifts of food, each helping to prepare a joyous meal that is savored by one and all. According to the custom, the first night is a barbecue, with the delightful scent of arrosticini and sausages filling the air. On the second night, all the women in town prepare over three hundred homemade pizzas in traditional ovens throughout the town. (In 2015, we were busy preparing the pizza dough when a terrible storm passed through the town. Everyone hurried into their homes for cover, but I was caught in the storm with two small children. I remember grabbing hold of a door knocker with one hand, while I tried to shield the children with my other arm. The wind was so strong, it almost lifted us into the air.) On the third and final night, *pasta fagioli* is served as the people dance and revel late into the night.

Over the years, there have been many additions to the menu, including some unexpected ones. A few years ago, for instance, I introduced the Philadelphia cheesesteak to the festival, which was met with great enthusiasm. Indeed, it was so popular that we prepared over five hundred sandwiches one year. My daughter-in-law began another tradition—a pancake breakfast. Although transporting enough maple syrup across the Atlantic Ocean has certainly introduced its own set of challenges, she does it with a full heart in order to see the smile on the faces of some of the town's most elderly members. She may not be Italian, but she has embraced the traditions and is much admired by the town.

The primary purpose of the *festa* of San Massimo is to raise money for the local church and public spaces, a mission that took on new significance after the 2009 earthquakes that left many of the mountain towns of Abruzzo in ruins. Our family home was devastated, and it took over a year to make it stable and secure. During the home repairs, my mother-in-law and most of the people in town were forced to live in tents provided by the Red Cross. Almost ten years later, with many other earthquakes following in recent years, the restoration of the town continues, including the church of San Massimo, dating back to the eighteenth century.

The idea of a community coming together to share its food is a tradition that is honored on an almost daily basis in Italy. It is the Italian way of life, and anyone familiar with Italian culture will not be surprised to hear that this tradition has also become the basis for various myths and legends. The Stone Soup story is one such legend, and it goes like this: There was a very poor village with very little food, and in this village lived an elderly woman who had a stone. She went to each villager and told them she could make a soup using just a simple, humble rock placed in a pot of boiling water—but only if each villager shared a scrap of food to add to the broth. And so these poor villagers handed over an onion, or a carrot, or some other humble food that this old woman then placed in her pot containing boiling water and her starter stone. Soon enough, this simple stew would become a delicious feast that all the townspeople could share.

The fable points up the importance of community and teaches us that while we may be poor and hungry alone, as long as we have friends and neighbors, we will never starve. There are other variations of this story, some of which involve a destitute traveler who arrives in a town with nothing but a rock. With cunning and guile, our downtrodden protagonist tricks the local townspeople into donating items that become a wonderful soup. The essential conceit is the same, although this version humorously casts the poor traveler as an unlikely hero.

The true origin of the Stone Soup story may never be known, but, like most myths and legends, it likely has a basis in reality. In fact, there is good reason to believe that it grew out of a very ancient recipe for *acquacotta*, which, translated from the Italian, literally means "cooked water." This dish was invented as a way to reuse stale bread by repurposing it into a broth that was enhanced with very basic vegetables. It is not difficult to see parallels between a stone being used as a soup starter and a rock-hard chunk of old bread. The origins of *acquacotta* likely trace back to the very poor inhabitants of the Tuscan region. Because of the scarcity of local industry, the men would often travel great distances and for long periods to find work. It is easy to picture a poor, humble traveler or farmer away from home for an extended time. He carries few supplies with him as he travels the rugged countryside, making his way up and down the interior tract of ancient Italy looking for work. Perhaps this lonesome traveler has an old pot suitable for boiling water over a humble fire. He happens upon a village, bringing with him only a large chunk of bread that has long since passed the point of freshness. Crumbs from this stale loaf will certainly serve to thicken the water he boils, but it would be pretty basic fare without some additional ingredients. So our traveler visits the townspeople, seeking scraps from their tables to add to his soup. They comply by sharing their basic vegetables, and soon the broth is thick from the old stale bread and hearty from the addition of the donated veggies. A pot of humble boiled water and bread is now a delicious meal to keep our traveler warm as he continues along his way.

Whether *acquacotta* is the inspiration for the Stone Soup fable may never be known for sure, but maybe it does not matter. I can think of a great many traditions and customs that our family followed that likely grew out of practicality. Italians have a certain way of taking true events and recasting them with humor and wit, all in the service of a good story. After all, just like good cooking, sometimes a story needs a little spice to make it more interesting.

To me, the Stone Soup fable contains a dash of truth that has been carefully nurtured. As the myth has been retold over the years, the ingredients have been modified by each storyteller, and, much like a family recipe, there are now many variations that derived from the original. Regardless, the most important part of the story remains. At the end of the Stone Soup fable, the villagers and the lonely traveler are hunkered over bowls of their delicious soup. Our traveler, though, is no longer a stranger. The act of cooking together has become symbolic of breaking down barriers, of people coming together over food. This is the essence of what we celebrate when we prepare meals for loved ones, and it is this spirit of togetherness, united by food in a greater cause, that is honored during each of our meals.

ABRUZZESE SEVEN VIRTUES SOUP

(Le Virtù Abruzzesi)

Serves 8–10 people

Soups are always a hearty meal in an Italian household. They also contain many "bits of this" and "bits of that," simply meaning whatever you have on hand. As I have mentioned before, waste in the kitchen is not acceptable. A special time of year when this philosophy is clearly apparent in Abruzzo is the beginning of May— May 1, to be exact, when *Le Virtù* is celebrated throughout the region. This incredible soup, consisting of nearly four dozen ingredients and needing two days of preparation time, is a labor of love and dedication to your family. Traditionally, you need to include seven legumes and beans, seven herbs and spices, seven vegetables, seven types of pasta, seven types of meat, olive oil, and plenty of aged cheese.

Mythological stories (or rumors), which the imaginative Abruzzesi are sometimes known for, talk about this soup as a marriage of old and new crops. Traditionally, the soup was also meant to bring back strength to the men who would be returning to the fields after a winter of relaxing, and to give strength to new mothers, since the springtime brought lots of new babies. By the beginning of May, many kitchen cupboards were running low of pulses and legumes from the previous year's summer crops, which had served the families well during the harsh winter. The significance of the number "seven" is meant to signify the seven days it took God to create the earth; it also references the virtues taught by the Catholic Church.

As I have mentioned before, meat was expensive and, when an animal was slaughtered, nothing was wasted. Whatever wasn't used immediately was somehow preserved for later consumption. This would include cheap cuts of meat, pigskin, ears, ham bones, and feet.

I remember my first May Holiday in San Massimo with my husband and his family. For days before the preparation, his grandfather Taddeo would chant in a loving way that it was time to clean the kitchen. He was referring to all the leftovers and forgotten preserves. Although preserves and any leftover food that was still edible were added, you also included the first crops of the spring, and, on occasion, some animals were slaughtered and divided among several families to add to the pot.

The women also had an exchange, so everyone only had to prepare one kind of pasta, rather than all seven. I remember them discussing which pasta they would make or what types of dry pastas they had left in their pantry for the exchange. (It was like the modern-day Christmas cookie exchange my daughter and daughter-in-law participate in every year.) Neighbors would also share and exchange other ingredients to help each other reach the magic "seven" numbers.

Over the years, the recipe has become sophisticated for modern taste buds and more appropriate for modern lifestyles, too. Using canned beans, for example, will reduce the preparation time from two days to a few hours. Plan on inviting the neighbors over and having lots of leftovers from this dish.

Ingredients

Staples:

1 cup olive oil

2 cups dry white wine

Salt, to taste

1 cup freshly grated Parmesan cheese

1 cup freshly grated Pecorino Romano cheese

Herbs and spices:

4 garlic cloves, chopped

½ bunch fresh parsley, chopped

½ bunch fresh thyme, chopped

¼ cup chopped fresh mint

3 bay leaves, whole

1 teaspoon black pepper

1 teaspoon nutmeg

Meats:

1 (1-pound) piece pancetta

1 Cornish hen or quail

½ pound beef, cubed

½ pound beef ribs

4 Italian sausages, casing removed

3 chicken legs or 1 pig foot

1 veal chop, on the bone

Vegetables:

3 large onions, chopped

3 carrots, chopped

1 fennel bulb, chopped

2 celery stalks, sliced

2 bunches spinach, chopped

½ head cabbage, shredded

5 (28-ounce) cans crushed tomatoes

4 fresh tomatoes, diced

Legumes and pulses (use canned beans, drained well):

½ cup chickpeas

¼ cup green peas

¼ cup lima beans

1 cup lentils

¼ cup kidney beans

¼ cup fava beans

¼ cup butter beans

Pastas:

¼ cup dry orzo

¼ cup dry spaghetti, broken into 1-inch pieces

¼ cup dry ditalini

½ pound dry tortellini

¼ cup dry pastina

¼ cup dry elbow macaroni

¼ cup dry orecchiette

1. In an extra-large stockpot, heat 1 cup olive oil and 4 chopped garlic cloves over medium heat. Add the meats, 2 cups dry white wine, and a pinch of salt, and sauté for 5–7 minutes. Add the onions, carrots, fennel, and celery, and continue to sauté for an additional 5 minutes.

2. In a separate stockpot, combine the spinach and cabbage with a pinch of salt, and generously cover with water. (You will be using this spinach-cabbage water throughout the recipe.) Bring to a boil and simmer for 20 minutes. Using a strainer, drain the spinach and cabbage (do not discard water), and add to stockpot with the meat.

3. To the stockpot with the meat mixture, add the crushed tomatoes, 6 cups of the reserved spinach-cabbage water, the parsley, thyme, mint, bay leaves, pepper, and nutmeg. Reduce the heat and add enough additional spinach-cabbage water to cover and fill the pot approximately three-fourths of the way full. Allow to simmer for 2 hours, stirring occasionally. Continue to add spinach-cabbage water, if needed.

4. Remove all the meat with bones, including hen or quail, and strip the meat away from the bones, discarding the bones. Return the meat to the pot. Add all the legumes and pulses, the four fresh diced tomatoes, and few pinches of salt to the pot.

5. *Prepare the pasta:* Add additional fresh water to the stockpot used for the spinach and cabbage, and bring to a boil. Add your dry pastas, except for the tortellini, and cook until al dente. Using a strainer, drain the pastas (do not discard the water) and add them to your soup pot. Finally, drop the tortellini into the boiling water and cook according to package instructions. Drain (reserve some of the water), and add to the soup pot. Add some pasta water if the soup is too thick to your taste. Add cheeses to the pot and mix thoroughly. After 4 hours of preparation, the soup is ready to serve.

SAFFRON AND POTATO MINESTRONE SOUP

(Minestra di Patate allo Zafferano)

Serves 4–6 people

Ingredients

Salt

4 cups russet potatoes (approximately 6–8 potatoes) peeled and diced

¼ cup olive oil

2 cups chopped Spanish onion

2 carrots, cut into ¼-inch-thick slices

2 celery stalks, cut into ¼-inch-thick slices

1 teaspoon saffron

4 cups dry cannarozzetti or ziti

¼ cup freshly grated Pecorino Romano cheese (optional)

Directions

1. Bring a pot of salted water to a boil, then add the potatoes and cook until al dente (approximately 20–25 minutes). Drain and set aside.

2. Heat the olive oil in a medium sauté pan, then add the onion, carrots, and celery, and sauté for 5–7 minutes. Remove and cool slightly. Add the saffron to the vegetables and mix thoroughly.

3. Bring a pot of water to a boil and cook the pasta until al dente, according to the package instructions.

4. As the pasta water begins to boil, add 8 cups of water and a generous pinch of salt to the pot used to boil the potatoes and bring to a simmer. Add the drained potatoes and continue to simmer over medium heat for 5 minutes. Add the sautéed vegetables and continue to simmer for another 5 minutes.

5. Drain the pasta well and add to the vegetable soup. Add the cheese, if using, and mix the pasta thoroughly with the vegetables. Transfer to a serving bowl and serve hot.

CHICKPEA AND PANCETTA SOUP

(Zuppa di Ceci e Pancetta dell'Aquila)

Serves 4–6 people

Ingredients

1½ cups dried chickpeas
(see Note)

2 bay leaves

1 rosemary sprig

1 tablespoon salt, plus
additional to taste

8 cups chicken stock

¼ cup olive oil

2 garlic cloves, chopped

1 Spanish onion, chopped

½ pound pancetta, cubed

2 cups quartered
cherry tomatoes

1 pinch red pepper flakes

Pasta (optional)

Directions

1. Soak the chickpeas in a bowl filled with cold water for at least 12 hours or overnight. Drain the chickpeas and place them in a saucepan, along with the bay leaves and rosemary. Cover with cold water and 1 tablespoon salt and bring to a boil. Reduce heat and simmer for 2 hours. Once cooked, drain and set the chickpeas aside.

2. Pour the chicken stock into a large stockpot and bring to a boil.

3. While waiting for the stock to boil, heat the olive oil and garlic in a sauté pan over medium heat. Add the onion and pancetta and sauté until the onion begins to brown, then add the tomatoes and pepper flakes, and continue to sauté.

4. Once the chicken stock comes to a boil, add the chickpeas and the pancetta mixture to the stockpot. Add a pinch of salt and simmer over low heat, partially covered, for 30 minutes. You can add some small dry pasta if a heartier soup is preferred. Ladle into bowls and serve.

NOTE
Canned chickpeas, rinsed thoroughly, can be substituted for the dried chickpeas; you will not have to give them the cold water bath.

BEETROOT AND FARRO SOUP

(Zuppa di Barbabietola e Farro)

Serves 6 people

Ingredients

½ head cabbage, chopped

¼ cup olive oil

4 garlic cloves, chopped

½ pound pancetta, diced

1 carrot, peeled and chopped

1 russet potato, peeled
and chopped

2 cups chopped beetroot

1 bay leaf

¾ cup farro

8 cups vegetable stock

Pinch of salt and black pepper

¼ cup freshly grated
Pecorino Romano cheese,
for garnish

Directions

1. Place cabbage in a saucepan and fill the pan with water. Bring cabbage to a boil, then simmer on low heat until ready to transfer to the soup pot.

2. In a large stockpot, heat olive oil and garlic over medium heat. Add the pancetta, carrot, potato, beetroot, and bay leaf, and sauté for 10 minutes. Place the farro in a colander and rinse several times under cold running water for 5 minutes.

3. Add the vegetable stock to the beetroot mixture in the pot and pour in the farro. Add a pinch of salt and black pepper, increase heat, and bring to a boil. Once boiling, add another pinch of salt, reduce heat, and simmer for 20–25 minutes. Drain the cabbage with a strainer and add to the soup pot. Ladle soup into bowls and garnish with cheese.

EGG PASTA AND PEA SOUP

(Zuppa di Quadrucci all' Uovo con Piselli)

Serves 4–6 people

Ingredients

For the pasta:

2 cups all-purpose flour,
plus more for dusting

3 large eggs

Olive oil

For the soup:

¼ cup olive oil

2 large Spanish onions,
chopped

2 cups peas

2 cups cubed pancetta

1 cup dry white wine

Pinch of salt

½ cup freshly grated
Parmesan or Pecorino Romano
cheese

Directions

1. *Prepare the fresh pasta:* Mound the flour in the center of a clean, large wooden board or flat work surface. Make a well in the center of the flour and add the eggs. Using a fork, beat the eggs together, then begin to incorporate the flour, starting with the inner rim of the well. As you expand the well, keep pushing the flour up to retain the well shape. (Do not worry if it looks messy.) When half the flour is incorporated, the dough will begin to come together. Start kneading the dough, using primarily the palms of your hands. Once the dough is a cohesive shape, set the dough aside, scraping up and discarding any dried bits of dough.

2. Continue kneading the dough for 10 minutes, dusting your board or work surface with additional flour as needed. The dough should be elastic and a little sticky. Put the dough in a bowl, spread olive oil around the dough mass, and cover with a kitchen cloth. Allow to rest for 30 minutes at room temperature before proceeding.

3. Cut the dough into four equal-sized pieces. Cover them with a clean kitchen towel and keep them covered when you are not handling the dough to prevent it from drying out. Working with one piece of dough at a time, dust the work surface and the dough with a little flour and press the dough into a rectangle 5 to 6 inches thick. Roll through the widest setting on the pasta machine. Fold the rectangle of dough in half, and roll it through again. Repeat the rolling and folding process a few more times, to knead and smooth the dough. Return the dough to the covering cloth and repeat with the remaining dough pieces.

4. Switch to the next available setting on the machine. Roll a dough strip through the machine with the short end first. Repeat with the remaining dough strips. Continue this process through the narrower settings, now rolling only once through each setting, until you get to the next-to-last setting and the dough strips are about as wide as the machine (6 inches).

5. Cut the dough horizontally into ¼-inch-wide strips, then cut vertically into ¼-inch squares. Set aside and cover with a dry table linen.

6. *Prepare the sauce:* Heat the olive oil over medium heat in a 6-quart stockpot. Add the onions and sauté for 5–7 minutes. Add the peas and pancetta and continue to sauté for 10 minutes. Add the white wine and continue to sauté, until the wine evaporates. Add 12 cups of water (or chicken stock) and a pinch of salt and boil for 20 minutes. Add fresh pasta squares and cook for a 2–3 minutes. (If using the dry orzo pasta shortcut, see Note below.) Remove from heat, garnish with cheese, and serve.

NOTE

If you'd like to take a shortcut, you can substitute ¼ pound dry orzo pasta instead
of making the fresh pasta. Simply add the dry pasta once the water in the stockpot has boiled for
10 minutes and allow to boil for an additional 10 minutes.

"This is a classic hearty soup, common throughout the towns at the base of the
Gran Sasso Mountains. Over the years, I have replaced the fresh-shelled peas with
frozen peas, and my son has replaced the fresh egg pasta with dry orzo pasta to save time.
Many times I hear people say that there is no time to cook the traditional way. That may
be true, but you can experiment and find shortcuts that are just as good. This recipe is a
perfect example of something old meets something new!"

——ELISA

NETTLES SOUP

(Zuppetta di Ortiche)

Ingredients

Salt

1½ pounds fresh nettles, or
spinach, escarole, or kale

¼ cup olive oil

2 cups pancetta, diced

1 large Spanish onion, chopped

6 cups chopped fresh tomatoes

3 garlic cloves, minced

Cooked small dry pasta
(optional)

Directions

1. Fill a 6-quart stockpot with 12 cups of water and 3 tablespoons of salt and bring to a boil. Rinse the nettle leaves well under cold running water and cut the stems with leaves into small pieces, about 2 inches long. Add to the boiling salted water and cook for a 2–3 minutes. Remove the leaves with a strainer and place in a glass bowl of cold water. Continue to boil the water in the pot.

2. In a large sauté pan, heat the olive oil over medium heat. Add the pancetta and onion, and sauté for 10 minutes. Next, add the nettles, tomatoes, and garlic, and continue to sauté for 10 minutes. Add the nettle mixture to the boiling water in the stockpot, mixing thoroughly, and continue to cook for 5 minutes. You can add some cooked small dry pasta if a heartier soup is preferred. Add salt to taste, then serve.

"Nettles grew wild throughout the countryside, and the men would pick them as they were returning home from a day in the fields. The nettle leaves are rich in vitamins, and this soup was always prepared for someone who had fallen ill, or for women who had recently given birth to help them regain their strength. Nettle leaves are not as easy to find in the United States, but if you do, be careful in handling them because they may prick you. Feel free to substitute spinach or escarole. My son has recently used kale leaves."

—ELISA

TOMATO POTATO SOUP

(Zuppa con Patate e Pomodoro)

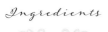

Ingredients

½ cup olive oil

5–6 garlic cloves, minced

4 medium potatoes, peeled and
cut into small cubes

Salt and black pepper

2 (28-ounce) cans crushed
tomatoes with basil

2 teaspoons tomato paste

½ cup chopped fresh parsley

¼ cup dry oregano

1 bay leaf

1 pound dry ditalini, mezzaluna pasta,
or mini ravioli (a family favorite)

½ cup heavy cream

¼ cup freshly grated Pecorino
Romano cheese

Directions

1. In a large saucepan, sauté oil and garlic over medium heat for 2–3 minutes. Gradually add the potatoes and a pinch of salt and pepper, and continue to sauté for 5–7 minutes.

2. In another large saucepan, place the crushed tomatoes, tomato paste, parsley, oregano, bay leaf, 2 tablespoons salt, and a pinch of pepper, and bring to a boil over medium heat. Stir occasionally to avoid burning. Add the potato mixture and 3 cups of water, reduce the heat, and simmer for 1 hour.

3. Bring a pot of water to a boil and cook the pasta until al dente, according to the package instructions. As your pasta is cooking, add the heavy cream to the tomato and potato mixture. (The potatoes should be soft, but not falling apart.) Add additional salt to taste. Drain the pasta well and add to the tomato and potato mixture. Ladle into bowls and garnish with the cheese.

Chapter Four

SIDE DISHES

(CONTORNI)

Abruzzese cuisine is the traditional cuisine of the area of Abruzzo, Italy. The cuisine draws on traditions in both pastoral and mountainous inland areas, and also along the coast. Among the foods most commonly used are bread, pasta, meat, cheese, and wine. The isolation that has characterized the region for decades has also ensured the independence and immutability of its culinary traditions.

Due to a predominating farming culture in Abruzzo, lamb dishes are a key part of Abruzzese cuisine. Such lamb and sheep dishes are mainly found in the mountainous areas of Abruzzo like my hometown. Sheep's milk ricotta is also used as an important source of Abruzzese cheese, and lamb intestines are often used as sausage casing.

Mountain goat meat is also common in Abruzzo. Other prominent ingredients and dishes in Abruzzese cuisine include truffles and mushrooms, garlic (especially local red garlic), extra virgin olive oil, and rosemary. Hot chili pepper, or pepperoncini as it is regionally known, is ubiquitous in much of Abruzzese cuisine and often used to add spice to dishes, while saffron is a specialty spice particular to L'Aquila, a neighboring city of my husband's hometown.

In addition to mushrooms, Abruzzese cuisine commonly employs "rustic" or "peasant" vegetation such as lentils, grass peas, and other legumes, artichoke, eggplant, wild asparagus, and cauliflower and, of course, potatoes. All of these fresh and seasonal ingredients are evident throughout my dishes.

As a young girl, preparing the side dishes and bread were usually my responsibility and tests as a cook by my mother and aunts. It wasn't until I proved to them that I could judge the baking time of bread by the crust and whether vegetables were cooked by their touch that they would give me more responsibility for the family meals.

EGGPLANT IN VINEGAR

(Melanzane Grigliate)

Serves 4 people

Ingredients

4 cups white wine vinegar

1 teaspoon sugar

1 tablespoon salt

4 eggplants

1 cup olive oil

¼ cup chopped fresh oregano

¼ cup red pepper flakes

Pinch of salt

Directions

1. In a large bowl, mix the vinegar, ¼ cup of water, sugar, and salt.

2. Remove skin from the eggplants and cut into ½-inch strips. Place sliced eggplant in the vinegar mixture and cover the bowl with plastic wrap. Set aside for 24 hours.

3. Drain eggplant and arrange on a clean kitchen towel. Roll up the kitchen towel, pressing firmly as you roll to really drain the eggplant of any remaining vinegar.

4. Place eggplant in a large serving bowl. Add the olive oil, oregano, red pepper flakes, and a pinch of salt. Toss to combine and serve.

"This is an excellent summertime picnic side dish and is delicious on sandwiches. You can also prepare a larger amount of eggplants to preserve for multiple uses."

—ELISA

MASHED CARROTS

(Purè di Carote)

Ingredients

8–10 carrots, peeled
and chopped

2 teaspoons brown sugar

¼ cup salted butter

1 cup heavy cream

¼ cup freshly grated
Parmesan cheese

Salt, to taste

Directions

1. In a large saucepan, place the carrots and cover with water. Add the brown sugar, bring to a boil over medium-high heat, and cook for 15–20 minutes, until carrots are soft. Remove from heat.

2. Drain carrots, return to the saucepan and mash with a masher. Add the butter and some of the heavy cream, place the pan over low heat, and warm the mashed carrots, stirring occasionally, for 10 minutes. Gradually add the remaining cream until the mixture is smooth. Add the cheese and a pinch of salt, and stir to combine thoroughly. Remove from the heat and serve warm.

POTATOES AND PEPPERS

(Patate e Peperoni)

Ingredients

6 potatoes, cut into
½-inch-thick slices

1 cup olive oil, plus more
if needed

Salt, to taste

3 yellow bell peppers, sliced

3 red bell peppers, sliced

Directions

1. Place the potato slices in a bowl of warm water and soak for 20–30 minutes prior to cooking.

2. In a medium-sized saucepan, heat the olive oil over high heat, add the potatoes, and sauté until they begin to brown. Add a pinch of salt and the bell peppers, and continue to cook for 15–20 minutes, until the potatoes are lightly browned and the peppers are soft, stirring often to keep the mixture from sticking to the pan and adding more oil, if necessary. Remove pan from the heat and transfer the potatoes and peppers to a serving bowl. Top with another pinch of salt and serve.

ZUCCHINI AND POTATO PARMESAN

(Parmigiana di Zucchine e Patate)

Serves 4–6

Ingredients

6 russet potatoes, peeled and cut into ½-inch slices

Olive oil

Salt

6 fresh zucchini, cut into ¼-inch slices

3 eggs

1½ cups *panna di cucina* or heavy cream

Pinch of black pepper

¼ cup chopped fresh basil

¼ cup chopped fresh parsley

2 cups grated Mozzarella cheese

1 cup freshly grated Parmesan cheese

½ cup breadcrumbs

NOTE

We use a round glass casserole dish with a lid or a 13 x 9 x 2-inch baking dish that we cover with foil. Ideally, you want to assemble the casserole in at least two layers; a smaller-size dish will yield three layers.

Directions

1. Place the potato slices in a large bowl of hot water and allow to soak for 2 hours.

2. Preheat the oven to 350°F and grease two baking sheets with olive oil.

3. Arrange potatoes on the prepared baking sheets. Drizzle more olive oil over the potatoes and generously sprinkle with salt. Bake for 15–20 minutes. Repeat this baking process with the zucchini, but omit the salt and bake for only 5 minutes. Whisk the eggs, *panna*, and black pepper in a bowl and set aside.

4. In a large casserole dish (see Note), arrange your ingredients in layers: Place a layer of potatoes on the bottom of the dish and brush with some egg mixture. Add a layer of zucchini and sprinkle with the herbs. Add a layer of the Mozzarella cheese and then add a layer of the Parmesan cheese. Repeat this layering process until the whole casserole dish is full. Pour the remaining egg mixture over the top, and, finally, add a layer of breadcrumbs. Bake, covered with a lid or foil, for 30 minutes.

"This has become one of my daughter Lily's favorite side dishes. It is made with *panna di cucina*, which is a dairy-based product found in Italy. Many of Mom's recipes call for this classic Italian kitchen staple, but since it is so difficult to find here, Mom uses heavy cream instead. Recently, I came across *panna* while surfing the Internet, and to our delight, it is now only a few clicks away. I often prepare this as an accompaniment to grilled steaks or a roast."

—FRANK

ITALIAN POTATO SALAD

(Insalata di Patate Freddo)

Serves 6–8 people

Ingredients

5 russet potatoes, peeled and each cut into 8 pieces

½ cup chopped fresh parsley

3 garlic cloves, chopped

¾ cup olive oil

3 tablespoons white wine vinegar

1 tablespoon dry white wine

1 teaspoon salt

1 teaspoon black pepper

Directions

1. Place the potatoes in a saucepan and fill with water. Bring water to a boil, then reduce heat, and simmer potatoes for 10–15 minutes, until tender. Drain potatoes immediately before they fall apart and set aside to cool.

2. When potatoes are cool, place them in a serving bowl. Add the parsley, garlic, olive oil, vinegar, wine, salt, and pepper, and toss gently. Refrigerate, covered with plastic wrap, overnight. Serve at room temperature.

"This is another summertime picnic favorite. On our summer holidays, we would often take day trips high up on the Gran Sasso Mountain to visit either the Campo Imperatore or the Madonnina Grotto on the Prati di Tivo. For as long as I can remember, we would have these family reunions. We would have a caravan of cars and, when we reached our destination, we would set out a buffet of cured meats, fresh breads, preserves, cheese, and dishes like this salad. The Campo Imperatore is historically important, but it is also famous for the many cattle farms in the area that sell fresh meat and have barbecue pits available to prepare the meat yourself. The Gran Sasso Mountains have so much to offer. Lately, unfortunately, they have been the site of many earthquakes, challenging the lives of those living in the towns at the base of the mountains."

——FRANK

BREAD AND PECORINO DUMPLINGS

(Pallotte Cacio e Ovo)

Serves 4–6 people

Ingredients

2 cups stale homemade Italian or ciabatta bread cubes

1 cup whole milk

Pinch of salt and black pepper

2 cups freshly grated Pecorino Romano cheese, plus more for garnish

1 egg

¼ cup finely chopped fresh parsley, plus more for garnish

¼ cup finely chopped fresh basil

1 ¾ cups olive oil

3 garlic cloves, chopped

1 large onion, sliced in half

2 (28-ounce) cans crushed tomatoes

2 whole basil leaves, for garnish

Directions

1. *Prepare the dough:* Place bread cubes and milk in a bowl and allow the bread to soak for 15 minutes. Drain the bread in a strainer and press out any excess milk. Discard the milk. In a large bowl, combine the bread, salt and pepper, cheese, egg, and the chopped parsley and basil, and mix with your hands to form a dough. Place the dough in a bowl and refrigerate, covered with plastic wrap, for 30 minutes.

2. While the dough is chilling, *prepare your sauce:* In a large sauté pan, heat ¼ cup of the olive oil over medium heat, then add the garlic and sauté for 5–7 minutes, until garlic begins to brown. Add both halves of the onion, the crushed tomatoes, and the basil leaves, then reduce the heat, and simmer for 30 minutes, stirring occasionally.

3. Place the remaining 1½ cups of olive oil in a saucepan and heat over medium-high heat. Take the dough out of the refrigerator, and form a fist-sized piece into a ball equal to the size of a small orange. Drop 2–3 balls at a time into the hot oil (do not crowd the pan) and fry for 3–4 minutes until golden brown. Remove the balls from the oil and place them on a paper towel–lined wire rack to absorb excess grease. Cook the remaining dough in the same way.

4. Place the cooked balls in the sauce, then reduce the heat to low and simmer, covered, for 20 minutes. Remove pan from the heat and garnish with additional parsley, basil leaves, and cheese. The dumplings can be served straight from the sauté pan or on a serving dish, for a more formal presentation.

BROCCOLI PANCETTA SALAD

(Insalata di Broccoli e Pancetta)

Serves 4–6 people

Ingredients

¼ cup olive oil

1 cup cubed pancetta

1 cup mayonnaise

⅓ cup sugar

3 tablespoons white vinegar

6 cups fresh broccoli florets

½ cup chopped white onions

¼ cup white raisins

¼ cup chopped walnuts

Directions

1. In a small sauté pan, heat the olive oil over medium heat, then add the pancetta and sauté for 4–5 minutes, until lightly browned. Drain the pancetta on a paper towel.

2. In a small bowl, place the mayonnaise, sugar, and vinegar, and mix thoroughly. Refrigerate, covered with plastic wrap, until cold.

3. Rinse the broccoli in a strainer, then place in a serving bowl, along with the onions, raisins, and walnuts, and toss. Add the dressing and toss lightly. Garnish with the pancetta and serve immediately.

MOZZARELLA AND SPINACH PASTA SALAD

(Insalata di Mozzarella e Spinaci)

Serves 4–6 people

Ingredients

1 bunch fresh spinach, chopped, or 1 10-ounce package of frozen chopped spinach

½ cup olive oil

3 garlic cloves, chopped

1 pound dry penne pasta

2 cups halved cherry tomatoes

1 cup sliced black olives

½ cup sliced green olives

1½ pounds fresh Mozzarella balls

For the dressing:

½ small onion, chopped

1 (2-inch) piece celery

1 garlic clove, minced

2 tablespoons dried oregano

1 teaspoon dried basil

1 teaspoon sugar

1 teaspoon black pepper

¼ cup white vinegar

⅔ cup olive oil

Directions

1. Bring a saucepan filled with water to a boil, then add the spinach and boil for 10 minutes. Drain spinach and transfer to a sauté pan. Add the olive oil and garlic, and sauté for 5–7 minutes. Remove from the heat and allow the mixture to cool completely. Set aside.

2. Bring a stockpot of water to a boil for the pasta. Cook pasta al dente according to the package instructions. Drain pasta. Transfer to a large serving bowl and allow to cool completely. Set aside.

3. *Prepare the dressing:* Place the onion, celery, garlic, oregano, basil, sugar, black pepper, and vinegar in a blender or food processor, and blend, then slowly add the olive oil until the dressing is emulsified. Transfer to a bowl and refrigerate, covered with plastic wrap, until ready to use.

4. Add a little dressing to the pasta and toss to loosen the pasta. Add spinach and toss thoroughly. Add tomatoes, olives, and cheese balls, and toss to combine. Finally, add the dressing and toss thoroughly. Refrigerate the salad, covered, until cold. Remove from the refrigerator and toss again before using. Serve chilled.

EGGPLANT GRATIN

(Melanzane Gratinate)

Ingredients

1–2 eggplants, depending on size

1½ cups olive oil, plus more for brushing and greasing

Salt and black pepper

2 garlic cloves, chopped

1 onion, chopped

2 (28-ounce) cans crushed tomatoes

1½ cups freshly grated Mozzarella cheese

Freshly grated Parmesan cheese

Directions

1. Preheat the oven to 350°F.

2. Peel and cut the eggplant into ¼-inch-thick round slices. Line a baking sheet with parchment paper and arrange the slices on the sheet. Brush the tops with 1 cup of the olive oil and sprinkle with a pinch or two of salt. Bake for 15 minutes. Remove from the oven and set aside.

3. In a large sauté pan, heat the remaining ½ cup olive oil and garlic over medium heat, then add the onions and tomatoes and sauté for 7–10 minutes. Remove from the heat.

4. Grease a large gratin dish with a little oil. Assemble the dish in layers (ideally, depending on the size of your dish, you should have three layers of eggplant and two layers of crushed-tomato sauce, onions, and Mozzarella cheese): Arrange one-third of the eggplant slices on the bottom of the dish, then add a layer of the sauce, then a layer of half the onions, then a layer of half the Mozzarella cheese. Continue to layer with half of the remaining eggplant, and all of the remaining sauce, onions, and Mozzarella cheese in the same way, ending with a third layer of eggplant. Top the eggplant with some salt, black pepper, and a generous layer of the Parmesan cheese. Bake for 20–25 minutes, until the top bubbles, and serve straight out of the oven.

"This dish is a modern, gluten-free version of my Eggplant Parmigiana, without the traditional use of bread or the traditional frying method. As our family grows with new marriages, so do the habits and needs of these new members. So to respect their needs, I created this dish."

—ELISA

ZUCCHINI POLENTA LOAVES

(Tortino di Polenta e Zucchine)

Serves 6–8 people

Ingredients

2 zucchini, peeled and thinly sliced

½ cup olive oil, plus more for greasing the pan

3 fresh rosemary sprigs, leaves removed

Salt, to taste

1 cup cornmeal flour

¼ cup all-purpose flour

3 teaspoons baking powder

1 egg

1 cup boiling water

1 tablespoon salted butter

Directions

1. Preheat the oven to 350°F.

2. Line a baking sheet with parchment paper and arrange zucchini in rows. Drizzle half of the oil over the zucchini and then sprinkle the rosemary and salt on the zucchini. Bake for 10 minutes. Remove from oven, turn over the slices of zucchini, and return to the oven to bake for 10 more minutes.

3. In a large bowl, combine the flours, baking powder, pinch of salt, the rest of the oil and the egg and whisk together until thoroughly blended. In a small saucepan, bring 1 cup of water to a boil, whisk in the butter until melted, and add to flour mixture.

4. Remove zucchini from the oven and pat with some paper towels to soak up the oil. Place the zucchini in a bowl and mash with a masher. Fold the mashed zucchini into the flour mixture with a wooden spoon. Grease 6–8 mini loaf pans or a cast-iron biscuit pan with some oil and fill equally with the mixture.

5. Bake breads for 15 minutes. Remove from the oven and carefully turn out onto a clean towel. Transfer breads to a wire rack and allow to cool.

"When I first moved to San Massimo after I married Francesco, I discovered that the women of his town often used cornmeal for making their bread. They also had access to many green vegetables. They would serve this dish with stews."

—ELISA

ITALIAN EASTER PIE

(Torta di Pasquale)

Serves 4–6 people

Ingredients

For the crust:

2½ cups all-purpose flour

¼ cup salted butter, cut into small pieces

¼ cup lard, cut into small pieces

½ teaspoon baking powder

3 eggs

Dash of lemon juice

2 tablespoons milk

For the filling:

6 eggs

3 cups Ricotta cheese

2 cups shredded fresh Mozzarella cheese

1 cup freshly grated Parmesan cheese

2 cups freshly grated Pecorino Romano cheese

2 cups cooked broccoli rabe

1 cup finely chopped fennel

1 small onion, chopped

¼ cup chopped fresh parsley

2 garlic cloves, minced

1 cup cubed pancetta

1 cup cubed prosciutto

1 cup cubed soppressata

1 cup cooked Italian sausage, crumbled

¼ teaspoon ground nutmeg

Pinch of salt and black pepper

Directions

NOTE

If you do not want to prepare the dough by hand, you can use an electric stand mixer with a dough hook.

1. *Prepare the crust:* Mix the flour, butter, lard, and baking powder, and form the flour mixture into a mound in the center of a large wooden or marble-like surface. Make a well in the center and add 2 eggs and the lemon juice to the well. Using a fork, beat the eggs and lemon juice together. Then begin to incorporate the flour, starting with the inner rim of the well. Gradually add some water, a few tablespoons at a time, until a silky dough begins to form. Continue to knead the dough, adding more water until you have a consistent dough ball. Wrap the dough ball with plastic wrap and place it in the refrigerator for 30 minutes.

2. Preheat the oven to 350°F.

3. While the dough is resting, *prepare the filling:* In a large bowl, beat the 6 eggs, then add all the remaining filling ingredients, one at a time, mixing each thoroughly before adding the next, until the filling is a uniform consistency.

4. Divide the chilled dough into three equal-sized parts. Combine two parts of the dough and roll out enough dough to cover the bottom and sides of a 13 x 9 x 2-inch glass baking dish, with an extra 1 inch of dough for the sides. Reserve the excess dough.

5. Fill the pie crust with the filling mixture. Roll out the third piece of dough on a flour-covered surface and cover the top of the filling, trimming excess. Crimp the two dough edges together tightly, using a fork.

6. Take the reserved dough and roll it out. Cut two dough strips and form a cross on the top of the pie. In a small bowl, whisk together the remaining egg and the 2 tablespoons of milk and brush over the top of the pie, including the cross and the edges. Make four slits in the top of the pie.

7. Bake in the center of the oven for 30 minutes, then reduce the heat to 300°F and bake for 40–45 minutes more, until golden brown. Remove from the oven and allow to cool for 4–6 hours before serving. Serve at room temperature.

TORTA DI PASQUALE: A LOCAL TRADITION

As with most Italian dishes, there are many variations of this pie throughout Italy. It all depends on regional harvests and what fresh ingredients are available. This dish is prepared during the Easter holidays in thanks to God for all he provides. In my hometown, we use cured meats and cheese, very common specialties among the farming communities in the Gran Sasso Mountain region. The use of cured meats thanks God for watching over the preservation of these meats throughout the winter months when fresh meat is scarce. The use of fresh cheeses thanks God for the new crops of the spring and the birth of young animals during the winter months. Some regions of Italy incorporate thirty-three ingredients to honor every year God gave us his son on earth. It is also full of various meats to celebrate the end of fasting during the Lenten season.

—ELISA

STUFFED EGGPLANT

(Melanzane Ripiene)

Serves 6 people

Ingredients

3 small eggplants

1¾ cups olive oil

2 garlic cloves, chopped

1 pound prosciutto, chopped

2 Spanish onions, chopped

1 cup Italian breadcrumbs

1 pound Mozzarella cheese, grated

¼ cup chopped fresh parsley

1 teaspoon salt

Pinch of black pepper

1 cup dry white wine

2 eggs, beaten

Directions

1. Cut the eggplants in half from the top to the base. Remove seeds with a paring knife. Using a spoon, scoop out the remaining flesh and place in a large mixing bowl. Set eggplant shells aside until ready for use.

2. Preheat the oven to 350°F.

3. *Prepare the stuffing:* Heat ¾ cup olive oil and the garlic in a large sauté pan over medium heat, then add the eggplant flesh, prosciutto, and onions, and sauté for 5–7 minutes. Transfer mixture to a bowl and allow to cool. When cool, add the breadcrumbs, cheese, parsley, salt, black pepper, ½ cup white wine, and eggs and mix thoroughly.

4. Spoon the stuffing into the eggplant shells. Place the stuffed eggplants into a baking pan and drizzle with 1 cup olive oil and remaining ½ cup wine. Bake for 45 minutes to 1 hour, until eggplant is tender to the touch. Remove from oven and transfer to a serving platter. Serve immediately.

NOTE

You can also modify this recipe to prepare the stuffed eggplant with a delicious sauce. Instead of slicing the eggplant, cut off the top and hollow out the centers. Follow the directions above, and place the stuffed eggplants in a large stockpot. Add a whole onion and 4 (28-ounce) cans of crushed tomatoes, and cook over medium heat for 1½ hours.

POTATO AND MUSHROOM TIMBALLO

(Timballo di Patate e Funghi)

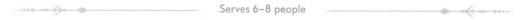

Serves 6–8 people

Ingredients

2 pounds russet potatoes

½ cup olive oil

2 garlic cloves, chopped

1 pound fresh mushrooms, sliced

½ cup dry white wine

¼ cup chopped fresh parsley

¼ cup chopped fresh oregano

Pinch of salt and black pepper

2 eggs

½ cup freshly grated
Mozzarella cheese

¼ cup freshly grated Fontina cheese

¼ cup freshly grated
Pecorino Romano cheese

2 cups *panna di cucina* or heavy cream

1 tablespoon unsalted butter

Directions

1. Preheat the oven to 400°F.

2. Peel and thinly slice potatoes using a mandolin or a sharp knife. Place in a bowl filled with cold water and set aside for at least 1 hour.

3. Heat the olive oil and garlic in a sauté pan over medium heat, then add the mushrooms, wine, parsley, oregano, and a pinch of salt and pepper, and simmer for 5–10 minutes, until tender and the wine has evaporated.

4. In a bowl, beat the eggs, then add the cheeses and *panna* or cream, and blend thoroughly until smooth.

5. Grease a 13 x 9 x 2-inch baking pan with the butter and line with parchment paper.

6. *Assemble the timballo in layers:* Line the bottom and sides of the pan with a layer of potato slices; layer half the mushrooms over the potatoes; then top with half the cheese mixture. Repeat with another layer of potatoes, the remaining mushrooms, and the remaining cheese. Finally, top with the remaining potatoes.

7. Bake for 45 minutes or until the potatoes are tender. Remove from the oven and let stand for 5–10 minutes. Flip the timballo over onto a serving platter or a wooden board and unmold, just like my classic timballo. If you plan to serve the timballo in the pan, do not use the parchment paper to line the pan.

Chapter Five

MEATS AND SEAFOOD

(*SECONDI PIATTI*)

TIME TO MAKE THE SAUSAGE

Traditions are customs or beliefs that are passed down from one generation to another. Much of this book has been dedicated to my Italian food traditions and how they both shaped my new life in America and were altered by my life here, too. The tradition of making sausage, in particular, is an example of how my country of origin influenced my thinking about food in my new homeland. And, certainly, the practicalities of living in America caused me to rethink how I prepared traditional foods.

Every February, my brother Nicola and I make sausage, something we have done every year since we were children. When we do this now, it is a good excuse for us to be in each other's company, perhaps enjoy a few glasses of wine together, and to tell old stories in our native tongue. As we approach our golden years, I know Nicola wishes I would retire so we could have more time to spend together. But he also knows how important the people that I work with are to me (I share my time with special needs people, helping them with daily tasks, laundry, cooking, etc.), so he is willing to share my time as long as I honor our February date.

Making sausage is a communal experience, with friends and in-laws helping to grind the meat, stuff the sausage, and tie off the links. I must say that, after more than fifty years, our family has formed quite an efficient assembly line of operations. The work comes naturally to our fingers, and this allows our minds to wander and our conversations to linger. It is not that our work requires no focus; it's just that the steps are so practiced that they are second nature to us. This is the beauty of traditions: Their familiarity makes them comforting. As is the case with most traditions in Italian culture—and it is certainly the case in our sausage making—they unite families, or at least serve as an excuse for the family to gather together.

There are certainly many humorous (some might say bizarre) customs associated with sausage making. According to certain members of our family, the work must always be started on a Monday after a full moon. There is also a certain order to the operation, and it must never be changed, lest the final product be ruined. Superstitions aside, sausage making was incredibly important for our family. Every year, our humble family would butcher one of our prized pigs. Because the meat was so valuable, we had to make sure it lasted as long as possible. So this particular tradition grew out of necessity. When we would gather the family members and work together to make sausage and dried and cured meats, it was done to ensure that we would have meat to eat throughout the remainder of the year. Sausage could be broken apart and the meat re-formed to make meatballs to be used with pasta or in soups. Links could be cooked whole and paired with the spring harvests of cabbage and cauliflower to form beautiful meals—some would call this peasant food, but I describe it more as traditional Italian countryside cooking. If our family was very careful about how we used our sausages, we could even make them last all the way into the next winter, just in time to make a new batch.

In America, certain cured meats, like pancetta and prosciutto, are considered luxury items. They can be brilliantly paired with fine cheeses, olives, and roasted peppers to make antipasti and other fine dishes. To our family, however, these preparations had nothing to do with luxury, and everything to do with making our foods last for the entire year. It was not unusual to have pancetta with bread for breakfast. If we were lucky, we might also have a fried egg.

Yet tradition does not necessarily mean that change is impossible. Fast-forward to today. The availability of fresh vegetables and other food products at grocery stores has made it less essential for us to practice the tradition of sausage making. Still, we continue on with this practice, partly because it is comfortable, partly because it is

what we have always done, but also because it keeps us connected to our roots.

There are many things we have changed about the way we make sausage. We no longer hang cured meats to dry by the hearth; instead, they hang in Nicola's garage. It might take a bit longer, but the result is the same. Some changes are for the better. For instance, the availability of sausage casing at the supermarket has eliminated the unsanitary practice of using the pig's intestine. We now purchase, rather than slaughter, our pig. And, although we prefer the hand-cranked machine, we now have an automated machine that extrudes the meat into the casing; it simply does this step more efficiently, once you know how to do it correctly. The point is that many of the smaller things about sausage making have changed for our family; even the reason we do it has changed. But that is the point. Traditions can change, adapt, and be adapted, yet still honor the past. If the spirit of the tradition lives on, it remains authentic and important. What a tradition means and why it is meaningful can be shared with the next generation, even if the particulars of the tradition are shaped and changed by circumstances and changing times.

I would like to imagine that my family will continue to make sausage into the future. I learned the traditional ways of making sausage first by watching the older members of my family, then later on by taking an active hand in the process. Now, my son Frank is learning the way we make sausage, and I hope that he will someday teach his children the lessons he has learned. Maybe he won't hang dried meats in his garage or basement, and perhaps he will never butcher and process a whole pig. Chances are that my children and their children will get most of their sausage from the grocery store; but chances are also good that they have learned that not all sausage is made in a factory, that there is still value in the hard work it takes to hand-produce food, and that any custom that results in the family spending time together can be a very good thing, indeed.

CHICKEN AND WHITE WINE

(Pollo con Vino Bianco)

Serves 4–6 people

Ingredients

2 pounds chicken
(thighs and legs)

¼ cup olive oil

1½ cups dry white wine

1 tablespoon salt

1 teaspoon black pepper

¼ cup chopped fresh parsley,
plus more for garnish

¼ cup chopped fresh oregano,
plus more for garnish

1 rosemary stalk, whole

2 garlic cloves, minced

2 scallions (including greens),
chopped

½ cup chicken stock

2 tablespoons salted butter

¼ cup heavy cream

Directions

1. Wash the chicken thoroughly under cold running water, pat dry, and place in a large, deep sauté pan with a lid. Pour the olive oil, then the white wine, over the chicken, and sauté over medium heat for 10 minutes. Add the salt, pepper, parsley, oregano, rosemary, garlic, scallions, and chicken stock, and bring to a boil, covered. Reduce heat, then simmer the chicken for 20–25 minutes, turning the chicken over occasionally.

2. A few minutes before the chicken is done, heat the cream and butter in a small saucepan.

3. When the chicken is cooked, remove the pan from the heat. Pour the cream mixture over the chicken and let it stand, covered, for 5 minutes before serving. Garnish with additional herbs and serve.

"As my children get older, they are willing to try new things without putting up a fight. Having lived in Asia for five years, and traveling the world, they have seen their fair share of unique dishes. This dish is something I throw together, usually on weeknights, when we are running short on time with many after-school obligations. It is a twist on my mother's classic roasted chicken recipe, a dish that graced many Sunday family dinner tables, but takes more time to prepare. I know chicken thighs and legs are not usually a crowd pleaser, but this dish is always a hit—everyone always asks for seconds. I like to serve this with a green vegetable and a simple risotto."

—FRANK

VEAL MARSALA

(Vitello al Marsala)

Serves 4 people

Ingredients

1 pound boneless veal

2 eggs

½ cup all-purpose flour

1½ cups salted butter

½ cup chopped fresh parsley

½ pound mushrooms, sliced

Pinch of salt and black pepper

¼ cup beef stock

¾ cup Marsala wine

Directions

1. Cut veal into thin slices, then pound into thin cutlets, ½ inch thick. Whisk eggs in a shallow bowl; place the flour in another shallow bowl. Dip each piece of veal into the eggs, then dredge in flour, coating both sides.

2. Heat 1 cup butter in a large sauté pan over medium heat. Add the cutlets and half the parsley, and cook until lightly browned on both sides. Transfer the cutlets to a plate and set aside. Place the mushrooms, a pinch of salt and pepper, and the remaining ½ cup of butter in the pan, and sauté for 4–5 minutes. Add the beef stock and Marsala wine and simmer until the mushrooms are tender (approximately10 minutes). Return cutlets to the pan and continue to simmer for 5 minutes more.

3. Remove cutlets from the pan and arrange on a serving platter. Pour the mushrooms and sauce over the veal. Garnish with the remaining parsley and serve.

SAUTÉED CHICKEN AND ONIONS

(Bocconcini di Pollo con Cipolla)

Serves 4–6 people

Ingredients

1½ pounds skinless, boneless chicken breasts

2 cups all-purpose flour

1 large Spanish onion, chopped

2 garlic cloves, minced

1 cup olive oil

1 cup dry white wine

Pinch of salt and black pepper

Directions

1. Wash the chicken thoroughly under cold running water and pat dry. On a clean surface, dice the chicken breasts. Place 1½ cups of flour in a bowl large enough to hold the chicken. Dredge the chicken in the flour and toss, coating it evenly on all sides.

2. Place the onion, garlic, and olive oil in a medium-sized sauté pan, and sauté over medium heat for 5–7 minutes. Add the chicken and continue to cook for 10 minutes more, stirring occasionally.

3. Add the wine and continue to cook, stirring occasionally, for 5 minutes. Add 1 cup of warm water and a pinch of salt and pepper and continue to cook for 15 minutes more. During the last few minutes, add the remaining ½ cup of flour and mix thoroughly to make a nice sauce. Remove from the heat, transfer to a serving bowl, and serve.

ON-THE-BONE PORK CHOP CUTLETS

(Cotoletta di Maiale)

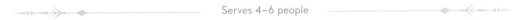

Ingredients

2 cups vegetable oil, for frying

8 thin bone-in pork chops

1 cup flour

1 teaspoon black pepper

1 teaspoon hot red pepper

1 teaspoon dried oregano

1 teaspoon dried parsley

Pinch of garlic salt

2 cups Italian breadcrumbs

1½ cups heavy cream

Directions

1. Heat the oil in a large, deep frying pan over medium-high heat.

2. *Prepare the chops for frying:* Rinse the chops under cold running water and pat dry. Pound the chops with a mallet until very thin, but with meat and bone still intact, and set aside. In a bowl large enough to hold one chop, combine the flour, black and red peppers, oregano, parsley, and garlic salt, and mix gently with a fork. Place the breadcrumbs in another bowl large enough in hold one chop. Pour the heavy cream into a third bowl of the same size.

3. Working with one chop at a time, place a chop in the heavy cream to coat, then dip into the flour, coating both sides. Shake off any loose flour. Re-coat the chop in heavy cream, then dip the chop into the breadcrumbs, turning over a few times, to cover completely. Transfer to a plate and coat the remaining chops in the same way.

4. *Fry the chops in batches:* Place 2–3 chops in the hot oil (do not overcrowd the pan) and fry on each side for 4–5 minutes, until cooked through. (To check for doneness, make a small incision at the center of the chop and make sure the meat is not pink. Transfer the chops, as cooked, to a paper towel–lined baking sheet and keep warm in a low oven. Fry the remaining chops and keep warm.

5. When all the chops are cooked, transfer to a serving platter and serve.

"Like many modern households, ours consist of two parents who work and two children who attend different schools. Add four or five extracurricular activities, and the first Saturday morning of the month is spent designing a driving schedule for the upcoming month. In our house, with all our pickups, drop-offs, and tag teaming as parents, I still seem to be the first one home, so, naturally, I like to get dinner started. Usually it's late, so I try to prepare something that can be ready within thirty minutes.

"One dish that Mom prepared often when I was young was breaded pork cutlets. Personally, I never cared for them because they always seemed dry, which I find is the case with many pork dishes. I seldom dared to challenge Mom's method of preparation because I knew she was following tradition. However, on the odd occasion when I was feeling strong and there was no wooden spoon in sight, I would tell her, 'Mom, these are dry.' Her response would be, 'Well, this is a recipe from your father's town.' Over time, Mom retired this dish, and when it came to cutlets, she turned to chicken. "As my wife and I continued to struggle to put a variety of healthy, quick, and easy dishes on the dinner table for our children every night, I decided to resurrect the pork chop. After several attempts at altering Mom's recipe, I finally came up with a dish that had everyone reaching for seconds. The secrets—heavy cream and a double breading. I usually serve this with some steamed asparagus and potatoes or broccoli rabe."

—FRANK

STEAK ON THE GRILL

(Bistecca alla Griglia)

Ingredients

2½–3-pound Porterhouse steak,
at room temperature

2 cups olive oil

Salt

¼ cup chopped fresh
rosemary leaves

¼ cup chopped fresh
parsley leaves

NOTE
*Sautéed peas and
a simple salad are ideal
accompaniments to
this steak.*

Directions

1. Place the steak in a large plastic zipper bag and add 1 cup of olive oil and about 1 teaspoon of salt. Seal the bag and refrigerate. Let the steak marinate for 1–2 hours before grilling.

2. Place the rosemary, parsley, 2 teaspoons of salt, and 1 cup of olive oil in a blender, and blend to form a dressing. Transfer to a measuring cup or a small bowl, and set aside.

3. Prepare the grill, and cook the steak on the grill to your liking. Transfer the steak to a plate and let it stand for 5 minutes. With a sharp steak knife, slice the steak, but do not detach it from the bone. Transfer to a serving platter, drizzle with the dressing, and serve.

PORK STEW

(Spezzatino di Maiale)

Serves 4–6 people

Ingredients

2 garlic cloves, chopped,
plus more for garnish

½ cup olive oil

2–3 pounds pork roast, cut into
cubes (see Note)

1 tablespoon salt, plus more to taste

Pinch of black pepper,
plus more to taste

¼ cup chopped fresh parsley,
plus more for garnish

2 Spanish onions, chopped

2 carrots, cut into
¼-inch-thick slices

2 celery stalks, cut into
¼-inch-thick slices

3 cups Montepulciano
d'Abruzzo red wine

3 cups chicken stock

1 bay leaf

¼ cup all-purpose flour

Directions

1. In a large sauté pan, sauté the garlic in the olive oil over medium heat until the garlic is golden. Add the pork, salt, pepper, and parsley, and sauté until the pork is brown, 4–5 minutes more. Add the onions, carrots, and celery, and sauté for a few minutes more.

2. Stir in the red wine and cook until the wine has evaporated (approximately 5 minutes). Add the chicken stock and bay leaf, and bring to a boil. Reduce the heat to the lowest setting and simmer, covered, stirring occasionally, for 2 hours. Add more wine or warm water, as needed, if the stew gets too thick. Add salt and pepper to taste. Shortly before the end of the cooking time, ladle a cup of the pork juices into a glass bowl, whisk in the flour, and pour the mixture back into the stew, stirring to combine.

3. When the stew is ready, remove the pan from the heat and transfer the stew to a serving bowl. Garnish with parsley and garlic cloves, and serve.

NOTE

*If you use a piece of pork roast on the bone,
be sure to add the bone to the pan for flavor.*

"This dish is reserved for the weekends, since it takes two hours of cooking time to prepare. I usually make some fresh bread while it is cooking because it is the perfect accompaniment for this stew. If you are looking for an alternative, either polenta or mashed carrots make a good choice."

—ELISA

BEEF AND PEPPER STIR-FRY

(Bistecca di Manzo e Peperoni)

Serves 4 people

Ingredients

1 cup flour

Salt and black pepper, to taste

2 pounds lean sirloin steak, cut into
½-inch slices

¼ cup olive oil, plus more for sautéing

3 cloves garlic, chopped

2 yellow onions, chopped

2 red bell peppers, sliced

2 green bell peppers, sliced

¼ cup dry white wine

2 (28-ounce) cans crushed tomatoes, or
4–5 cups chopped fresh tomatoes

¼ cup chopped fresh parsley

1 tablespoon chopped fresh oregano

¼ cup chopped fresh basil

Directions

1. Place the flour and a pinch of salt and pepper in a bowl, and mix thoroughly with a fork. Rinse the steak under cold running water, then pat dry and add to the flour, tossing to coat. Heat ¼ cup oil and the garlic in a large saucepan over medium heat, then add the sirloin and sauté for 5–7 minutes. Transfer the sirloin to a plate and set aside.

2. Add 2–3 tablespoons more oil to the pan, add the onions and bell peppers, and sauté for 3–4 minutes. Reduce heat to low. Return the sirloin to the pan, stir in the wine, and sauté for 3–4 minutes. Add the tomatoes and herbs. Partially cover the pan with the lid and continue to simmer, stirring occasionally, for 45–60 minutes. Add salt and pepper to taste. Remove the pan from the heat, transfer the stir-fry to a platter, and serve.

CHICKEN SALTIMBOCCA

(Saltimbocca di Pollo)

Serves 2 people

Ingredients

2 boneless, skinless chicken breasts

1 cup dry white wine

4 tablespoons salted butter

1 cup chopped fresh parsley,
plus more for serving

2 tablespoons all-purpose flour

2 garlic cloves, minced

½ cup olive oil

1 tablespoon salt

1 teaspoon black pepper

½ pound prosciutto, thinly sliced

1 dozen fresh sage leaves

½ pound fresh Mozzarella cheese,
thinly sliced

Directions

1. Preheat the oven to 350°F.

2. On a cutting board, butterfly each chicken breast (slice horizontally through the center but keep the breast in one piece, then open out like a book). Pound the breasts lightly with a mallet to tenderize. Set the chicken aside.

3. *Prepare the sauce:* Combine the wine, butter, parsley, and flour in a small saucepan. Bring to a boil over medium heat, stirring occasionally. Reduce heat to low and continue to simmer until ready to use.

4. In a large, ovenproof skillet (preferably a cast-iron skillet), sauté the garlic in the olive oil over medium heat. Add the chicken and sauté for 2–3 minutes on each side, until lightly browned. Remove pan from the heat.

5. Season the chicken with salt and pepper. Place 2 slices of prosciutto on each chicken breast. Place 1–2 sage leaves on top of the prosciutto, then top with slices of cheese. Pour the sauce into the skillet (avoid pouring the sauce on the chicken). Transfer the skillet to the oven and bake the chicken for 15–20 minutes, until the cheese is melted and the chicken is cooked through.

6. You can serve your chicken straight from the skillet, or transfer the chicken to a serving platter and ladle the sauce over the breasts. Garnish with sage and parsley.

NOTE

This recipe can be doubled or tripled for a larger party. When a skillet will not hold all the breasts for baking, simply brown the chicken, one or two at a time, then transfer them to a casserole dish for baking.

BEEF AND POLENTA

(Polenta con Manzo)

Serves 4–6 people

Ingredients

For the beef:

3 garlic cloves, minced

½ cup olive oil

2 pounds chuck steak, cut into 2-inch cubes

Salt and black pepper, to taste

2 Spanish onions, sliced

2 tablespoons tomato paste

4 cups beef stock

2 cups chopped tomatoes

2 cups dry red wine

2 tablespoons chopped fresh rosemary leaves

2 fresh sage leaves

Freshly grated Pecorino Romano cheese, for garnish

For the polenta:

2 teaspoons salt

1 cup yellow Italian polenta

2 teaspoons olive oil

Directions

1. *Prepare the beef:* In a large sauté pan, sauté half the garlic in ¼ cup of olive oil over medium heat. Add the beef, with a pinch of salt and black pepper, and sauté for 3–4 minutes. Remove pan from the heat and set aside.

2. In a separate large sauté pan, place the remaining ¼ cup of olive oil and the onions, and sauté over medium heat until the onions are tender (approximately 5–7 minutes). Add the tomato paste and continue to sauté for 2–3 minutes. Add the stock, tomatoes, and red wine, and mix thoroughly. Add the beef mixture, top with the rosemary and sage, and add salt and pepper to taste. Reduce heat to very low, and simmer, covered, for 1½ hours, until the meat is cooked through.

3. *Prepare the polenta about 20 minutes before the beef is fully cooked:* Bring 3 cups of water to a boil in a large stockpot. Add 2 teaspoons of salt and gradually whisk in the polenta. Reduce heat to low and cook, stirring constantly, until the mixture thickens and the polenta is tender but still very loose and creamy, about 20–25 minutes. Turn off heat. Add the olive oil and mix thoroughly.

4. Transfer the polenta to individual pasta bowls and ladle the beef over the polenta. Garnish with some fresh Pecorino Romano cheese and serve.

"This is a winter favorite, especially on a snowy day when you are sitting by a wood-burning stove or fireplace. I recall my younger days of preparing the polenta in the fireplace over some coals. It is the fondest memory of my childhood in the kitchen with my mother. This dish warms the stomach, heart, and soul!"

—ELISA

SAUTÉED VEAL CHOPS

(Braciola di Vitello Saltata)

Serves 4–6

Ingredients

3 garlic cloves, chopped

1 cup olive oil

6–8 bone-in veal chops or pork chops,
pounded to 1 inch thick

1 large yellow onion, chopped

3 carrots, peeled and cut into ¼-inch-
thick slices

3 celery stalks, cut into ½-inch-thick
slices

Pinch of salt and black pepper

½ cup all-purpose flour

½ cup chopped fresh parsley

½ cup chopped fresh basil

2 cups crushed fresh tomatoes or
1 (28-ounce) can crushed tomatoes

Directions

1. In a large saucepan, sauté the garlic in the olive oil over medium heat for 2–3 minutes. Add the veal chops, onion, carrots, and celery, and sauté for 4–5 minutes more. Add a pinch of salt and pepper. Reduce heat to low, then add the flour, parsley, basil, and 1 cup of water, and sauté for a few minutes more, turning chops over, so they sauté evenly. Add the crushed tomatoes and an additional ½ cup of water. Increase heat to medium, and continue to cook for 20–25 minutes, until the veal is cooked through (make a small incision at the center of the chop and make sure meat is not pink and carrots and celery are tender. Serve immediately.

"You can serve this dish over rice as a *secondo* (entrée)
with a simple salad and fresh baked bread, or use some
of the sauce to serve over pasta."

—ELISA

CHICKEN INVOLTINI

(Involtini di Pollo)

Serves 4–6 people

Ingredients

Salt

3 bunches broccoli rabe

½ cup olive oil

3 garlic cloves, quartered

2 tablespoons salted butter

2 cups chopped mushrooms

2–4 red bell peppers,
cut into strips

1 large fresh Mozzarella ball

3 skinless, boneless chicken breasts

Black pepper

½ cup chopped fresh parsley,
plus more for serving

½ prosciutto, thinly sliced

1 cup dry white wine

½ cup all-purpose flour

1 cup chicken stock

Directions

1. *Prepare the broccoli rabe:* Bring a large pot of salted water to a boil, then add the broccoli rabe and boil for 10 minutes, until tender but still firm.

2. Meanwhile, in a large sauté pan, place ¼ cup of olive oil and the garlic, and sauté over medium heat until the garlic is lightly browned. When the broccoli rabe is ready, drain, add to the garlic mixture, and sauté for 5 minutes more.

3. *Prepare the mushrooms and peppers:* In a medium sauté pan, heat ¼ cup of olive oil and the butter over medium heat, then add the mushrooms, peppers, and a pinch of salt, and sauté for 10–12 minutes, until the peppers are tender.

4. Drain the Mozzarella ball. Cut the ball in half, then cut each half into three equal-sized slices.

5. Cut each chicken breast horizontally into 3 slices for a total of 9 pieces. Pound each slice with a mallet and flatten into a cutlet. Lay cutlets on a clean surface. Divide broccoli rabe evenly among the cutlets, placing a mound in the center of each cutlet. Top each cutlet with a slice of cheese, then spoon mushrooms and peppers over the cutlets, dividing the mixture evenly. Sprinkle the cutlets with salt, black pepper, and ¼ cup of chopped parsley.

6. Working with one cutlet at a time, roll up the cutlet, beginning with a narrow end. Depending on the size of your prosciutto pieces, lay 1 or 2 pieces of prosciutto on your work surface (if you use 2 pieces, overlap them). Place the rolled chicken at a narrow end and roll up the chicken in the prosciutto. Secure the roll with some toothpicks to keep it together. Roll up the remaining cutlets in the same way.

7. Place a little wine in one bowl and the flour in another bowl. Dip each piece of chicken in wine first, rolling to cover, and then roll in the flour.

8. Heat 3 tablespoons of olive oil in a large sauté pan over medium heat, then place the chicken in the pan and sear evenly on all sides, for 2–3 minutes. Remove pan from the heat, reserving the drippings in the pan, and transfer chicken to a plate. Set aside.

9. Place the remaining wine, the chicken stock, and a tablespoon of flour in a bowl, whisk thoroughly, and add to the drippings in the saucepan. Return the chicken to the pan and simmer over medium heat, for 10–15 minutes, adding more stock, if needed, until an instant-read thermometer inserted into the center of the chicken roll registers 165°F. When the chicken is done, transfer the chicken rolls with tongs to a serving platter and pour the remaining pan juices over the chicken. Garnish with parsley and serve.

"There are many, many different versions of this dish, depending on the region of Italy and even the town where it is prepared. The main ingredients—chicken, prosciutto, and cheese—are usually present in most versions. However, the vegetables used for this dish vary, based on what is on hand at the time or even what is left over from the previous day's meal. Waste was forbidden in my mother's kitchen because there were many times we did without, so we always found a way to recycle leftovers, if possible. This dish has always had a very nice presentation, so even though we may have wanted to impress our guests with a more expensive meat, like beef or veal, we tried to dress up our chicken the best way we could."

—ELISA

BEEF ROUND ROAST

(Rotolo di Manzo Arrosto)

Serves 6–8 people

Ingredients

2 cups olive oil

1 (3–4-pound) top round
roast of beef

1 cup white wine

3 carrots, peeled and
left whole

2 large onions, halved

4 celery stalks, cut in half

3 garlic cloves, chopped

Salt and black pepper, to taste

Directions

1. Heat the oil in a stockpot, over medium-high heat, until hot. Add the roast and sear on all slides, turning for even browning. Reduce heat to medium, add the wine, 4 cups of water, the carrots, onions, celery, and garlic, and simmer, covered, for 1½ hours.

2. Remove pan from the heat, and transfer the roast to a large plate. Pass all the vegetables and juices from the pan through a manual food mill (do not use a blender; it will change the color of your sauce). Return the roast and vegetables to the pot and allow to cool to room temperature. Refrigerate in the stockpot, covered, overnight.

3. Thirty minutes before serving, take the roast out of the refrigerator and preheat your oven to 350°F. Place the roast on a cutting board and carve into ¼-inch-thick slices. Arrange the roast slices in a large glass casserole dish and pour the sauce from the pan over the slices. Heat in the oven for 10–15 minutes, until juices bubble. Remove the casserole dish from the oven, transfer meat and sauce to a serving platter, and serve.

"You must prepare this dish one day before to allow the flavors of the meat and the sauce to meld. Sautéed peas or broccoli rabe go nicely here."

—ELISA

SAUTÉED SHORT BACK RIBS

(Cif e Ciaf)

Ingredients

¾ cup olive oil

3 garlic cloves, quartered

1 onion, chopped

2 carrots, chopped

1 long green hot pepper, chopped

1 celery stalk, sliced

2 pounds pork ribs, or beef ribs (cut from rack of ribs)

1 cup dry white wine

6–8 cups fresh crushed tomatoes or 3 (28-ounce) cans crushed tomatoes

¼ cup chopped fresh oregano leaves

1 sage leaf, plus more for garnish

Pinch of salt

Directions

In a large saucepan with a lid, heat ¼ cup of olive oil and the garlic over medium heat. Add the onions, carrots, hot pepper, and celery, then reduce heat to low, and cook for 10 minutes, stirring occasionally. Add ½ cup olive oil to a bowl. Roll each rib in the oil and place in the vegetable mixture in the pan. Add the wine and simmer, uncovered, for 15–20 minutes. Add the tomatoes, oregano, sage, and a pinch of salt. Cover and continue to cook for 20–25 minutes on low heat, stirring occasionally. Remove from the heat. Transfer ribs to a serving bowl and garnish with sage leaves.

"This dish was always reserved for the less popular cuts of pork and/or beef when animals were slaughtered. Today, I tend to use a full rack of ribs—short ribs, if they are available—to prepare this very, very simple entrée."

——ELISA

SEAFOOD PAELLA

(Paella di Pesce)

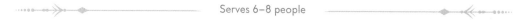

Serves 6–8 people

Ingredients

2 Spanish onions, chopped

3 garlic cloves, chopped

¼ cup olive oil, plus more for drizzling

2 (28-ounce) cans crushed tomatoes

2 bay leaves

1 pound fresh squid, sliced

1 pound cuttlefish, cut into pieces

1 pound lobster tail meat, cut into pieces

Salt, to taste

3 cups chicken stock

1 cup dry white wine

2 cups Arborio rice

2 dozen fresh mussels

2–3 dozen fresh clams

1 tablespoon saffron

Directions

1. In a large paella pan, sauté the onion and garlic in the olive oil over medium heat. Add the tomatoes and bay leaves, and simmer for 5 minutes. Add the squid, cuttlefish, lobster, and a pinch of salt, and cook, stirring, for a minute or so more.

2. In a saucepan, bring the chicken stock and wine to a boil. As it boils, add the rice to the fish mixture in the paella pan and blend thoroughly. Ladle three-fourths of the boiling stock over the rice and bring to a boil. Season the rice with more salt to taste. Reduce the heat to low and mix well, distributing rice evenly in the paella pan. Continue to cook the rice for 18–20 minutes, stirring occasionally.

3. While the rice is cooking, heat about 1 inch of water and a drizzle of olive oil in a separate sauté pan, then add the mussels. Steam until the mussels open, then transfer to the paella pan with a slotted spoon. Steam and transfer the clams in the same way. Take 1 cup of the clam water and whisk together with the saffron in a small bowl. Add to the paella pan, and simmer the mixture for 5 minutes more. Serve the paella directly from the paella pan.

"In the summer months, many in the mountain towns take a day trip to the beach nearby and purchase fresh fish for their meals. For me, a summer visit to San Massimo would not be complete without having my sister-in-law Franca's Seafood Paella, served al fresco in her garden with the Gran Sasso Mountains in the background. Franca loves to make fish dishes, and whenever she has *first-time* guests in her home, she prepares this dish. Throughout Abruzzo, whenever anyone has finished building a new home, it is traditional to cook a meal for all those who lent a hand to the project. Franca recently prepared this dish for just that purpose, when my son completed renovating a three-hundred-year-old home in the town. Actually, she will find any excuse to make it!

"In December 2013, my Francesco was losing his battle to cancer, but he knew his baby sister, Franca, was coming to spend Christmas with us. It was her first visit to America. Franca had cared for their mother until she died at the age of ninety-eight earlier that year, so it was always difficult for her to leave home. He was so excited to spend their first Christmas together in America, and she was so excited to share in the Christmas Eve tradition of the seven fishes that she decided to prepare this dish for him (it was always his favorite on his visits home). Franca arrived two days before the eve of Christmas and spent the morning of our traditional feast shopping for fish with my brother in the famous Italian Market of South Philadelphia. Unfortunately, that afternoon, Francesco took a turn for the worse, and while everyone was busy getting ready for the holiday, he slipped away quietly and lost his fight. Neither Franca nor Francesco got their wish that Christmas, but Franca went on to make the dish for the rest of us that night. She has told me since, that although it is still her favorite meal to prepare, she always sheds some tears while preparing it, but then laughs and smiles, remembering the happiness on her brother's face when she would make it for him when he would return home to San Massimo for a visit."

—ELISA

ITALIAN-STYLE CRAB CAKES

(Torte di Granchio)

Ingredients

4 cups lump crab meat

2 eggs

½ cup mayonnaise

2 tablespoons spicy mustard

1 tablespoon lemon juice

1 teaspoon anchory pasta

1 teaspoon celery salt

¼ cup chopped fresh basil

¼ cup chopped fresh parsley,
plus more for garnish

½ cup finely chopped red bell pepper

½ cup finely chopped Spanish onion

3 garlic cloves, minced

1 cup Italian-style breadcrumbs

2 tablespoons paprika

Generous pinch of crushed
red pepper flakes

Pinch of salt and black pepper

¼ cup freshly grated Parmesan cheese

¼ cup freshly grated
Pecorino Romano cheese

1 tablespoon red wine

Olive oil, for drizzling on the crab cakes

Lemon wedges, for garnish

Roasted Red Pepper Cream Spread
(page 227), for garnish

Directions

1. Preheat the oven to 350°F.

2. In a large bowl, combine all the ingredients (except the olive oil, lemon wedges, and roasted red pepper cream spread), and thoroughly mix by hand, gently pushing down with your palms at times to compact the mixture. Spoon the mixture into a biscuit cutter and press down with your fingers to pack the cake. Transfer the cake to an ungreased baking sheet. Make more crab cakes in the same way, arranging them 1 inch apart on the baking sheet.

3. Drizzle the cakes with some olive oil and bake for 20–25 minutes. Remove from the oven and transfer to individual plates. Garnish with my roasted red pepper cream spread, lemons wedges, and parsley, and serve.

NOTE

You can make mini crab cakes using a mini muffin tin.

CITRUS SALMON WITH PARSLEY

(Salmone Agli Agrumi)

Serves 4 people

Ingredients

1½ cups finely chopped
fresh parsley

1½ cups olive oil

1 cup lemon juice

3 garlic cloves, minced

Zest of 2 lemons

Zest of 1 lime

1 teaspoon salt

4 salmon steaks

Lemon and lime wedges,
for garnish

Directions

1. In a glass bowl, combine the parsley, oil, lemon juice, garlic, lemon and lime zests, and salt, and whisk with a fork. (You also can blend this mixture in a food processor, if you prefer.) Pour half the parsley mixture into a small bowl and refrigerate, covered.

2. Place each salmon steak on a piece of plastic wrap and generously brush the steaks on both sides with the remaining parsley mixture (discard any that you do not use). Wrap up the steaks in the plastic wrap and allow them to marinate in the refrigerator for 2–3 hours.

3. Preheat the broiler.

4. Remove the marinated salmon and the parsley mixture from the refrigerator. Transfer half the parsley mixture to a small bowl and set aside for garnish.

5. Unwrap the salmon steaks and place on a broiler pan. Broil for 3–4 minutes, then turn steaks over, brush with the remaining parsley mixture, and broil for 3–4 minutes more.

6. To serve, transfer the salmon to a serving platter or individual plates. Pour the reserved parsley mixture over the steaks and garnish with lemon and lime wedges.

"Our family tradition on Christmas Eve always features seafood, as is the tradition in many Italian households. When the children were younger, they were put off by the strange aroma of the seafood. My brother Nicola, however, would insist they take part in the tradition before they were allowed to open their Christmas gifts. This sometimes led to a restless dinner. My son wanted to introduce the Christmas Eve tradition to his children, but he wanted to change the experience. So he introduced these crab cakes to our table, hoping the kids would find them more appealing than fried smelts or baccalà."

—ELISA

BAKED SWORDFISH WITH TOMATOES, OLIVES, AND MUSHROOMS

(Pesce Spade al Forno con Pomodori, Oliva e Funghi)

Ingredients

¼ cup olive oil, plus 2 tablespoons

½ cup lemon juice

½ cup chopped fresh parsley

2 garlic cloves, chopped

Salt and black pepper, to taste

4 swordfish steaks

2 cups chopped Portabello mushrooms

1 cup minced green olives

2 cups chopped fresh tomatoes

Directions

1. Preheat the oven to 375°F.

2. In a large mixing bowl, place ¼ cup of olive oil, lemon juice, parsley, garlic, and a pinch of salt and pepper, and mix thoroughly. Place swordfish steaks into the bowl and toss to coat evenly. Allow the steaks to marinate, tossing occasionally, while preparing the sauce.

3. In a large sauté pan, heat the remaining 2 tablespoons of olive oil over medium heat, then add the mushrooms and olives, and sauté for 5–7 minutes. Reduce heat to low, add the tomatoes and a pinch of salt, and continue to sauté for 10 minutes more. Set sauce aside.

4. Remove the swordfish steaks from the marinade, reserving any marinade in the mixing bowl, and arrange on a grill pan. Bake the fish for 5–7 minutes. Remove pan from the oven, flip the steaks, and pour the reserved marinade over the steaks. Return steaks to the oven and bake for 10 minutes more. Transfer steaks to a serving platter or individual plates, ladle mushroom sauce over steaks, and serve.

"Throughout Abruzzo, it is common for a host to serve an antipasta of chilled seafood before the main meal. Chilled seafood has become popular at formal gatherings and celebrations, too. If monkfish is not available for this dish, any other white fish can be substituted."

—FRANK

CHILLED MARINATED FILLET OF FISH

(Filetto di Pesce Marinato Freddo)

Ingredients

3 tablespoons salted butter

1 cup all-purpose flour

1 cup olive oil, plus 5 tablespoons

1½ pounds thin monkfish fillets

Juice of 3 lemons

Pinch of salt and black pepper

¼ cup chopped fresh basil

8–10 fresh basil leaves, for garnish

Lemon wedges, for garnish

Directions

1. Melt the butter in a large sauté pan over medium heat. Place the flour and 2 tablespoons of olive oil in a glass bowl and whisk thoroughly to form a thick batter. Dip each fillet into the batter to coat evenly, then add to the sauté pan (do not overcrowd the pan) and fry, in batches, for about 2 minutes on each side. Transfer fish, as it's cooked, to a shallow baking pan.

2. Place 1 cup of olive oil, the lemon juice, and a pinch of salt and pepper in a mixing bowl, and whisk thoroughly. Pour over the fillets and refrigerate. Allow the fish to marinate in the mixture for 2–3 hours.

3. Before serving, *prepare a light pesto:* In a blender, place the chopped basil, 3 tablespoons of olive oil, and a pinch of salt and pepper, and blend. Remove fish fillets from the marinade and arrange on a serving platter. Drizzle the fish with the marinade and the pesto sauce, garnish with fresh basil leaves and lemon wedges, and serve.

SEA BASS POMODORO

(Spigola al Pomodoro)

Serves 4 people

Ingredients

½ cup olive oil

1 pound pancetta, cubed

1 Spanish onion, chopped

3 garlic cloves, minced

¼ cup Montepulciano d'Abruzzo red wine

1 (28-ounce) can crushed tomatoes

½ cup chopped fresh parsley

3 fresh basil leaves, chopped

¼ cup chopped fresh oregano

Pinch of salt and black pepper

4 sea bass fillets

Directions

1. In a medium saucepan, place 2 tablespoons of olive oil, pancetta, onion, and garlic, and sauté over medium heat until onions turn golden brown. Add the wine, tomatoes, half of the herbs, and a pinch of salt and pepper, and simmer the sauce, stirring occasionally, for 20–25 minutes.

2. Preheat the oven to 450°F and line a baking sheet with parchment paper.

3. Combine the remaining olive oil, the remaining herbs, and a pinch of salt and pepper in a shallow bowl, and mix thoroughly. Dip each fillet into the herb mixture to coat evenly and arrange on the prepared baking sheet. Drizzle the remaining herb mixture over the fillets and bake for 10 minutes.

4. Remove fillets from the oven and arrange on a serving platter or individual plates. Ladle the wine sauce over the fillets and serve.

SEAFOOD RISOTTO

(Risotto alla Pescatora)

Serves 4 people

Ingredients

5 cups fish or chicken stock

¼ cup olive oil

1 cup finely chopped Spanish onion

2 garlic cloves, minced

½ cup chopped Portobello
mushrooms

¼ cup chopped fresh parsley

2 cups Arborio rice

½ pound small scallops

½ pound shrimp, peeled

1 pound lobster meat,
cut into chunks

1 pound squid, cut into rings

2 cups chopped fresh tomatoes

Pinch of salt and black pepper

¼ cup freshly grated Parmesan or
Pecorino Romano cheese, for garnish

Directions

1. In a saucepan, heat the stock over low heat.

2. Heat the olive oil in a large sauté pan over medium heat, then add the onion and garlic, and sauté for 3–4 minutes. Add the mushrooms and parsley, and continue to sauté for 2–3 minutes. Add the rice, ladle enough stock over the rice to cover, and bring the mixture to a boil. Reduce heat to low, and continue to cook, occasionally adding more stock, one ladleful at a time, as stock is absorbed into the rice, for 10 minutes. Add the seafood, the remaining stock, tomatoes, and a pinch of salt and pepper, and cook for about 10 minutes more, until liquid is absorbed and the seafood is cooked.

3. Remove pan from the heat and transfer to individual bowls. Garnish with cheese and serve immediately.

SHRIMP AND SCALLOP CASSEROLE

(Gamberi e Capesante Casseruola)

Serves 4–6 people

Ingredients

2 pounds fresh shrimp

2 pounds fresh scallops

4 garlic cloves, minced

2 tablespoons salted butter, melted

2 cups heavy cream

½ cup freshly grated Parmesan cheese

½ cup freshly grated Pecorino Romano cheese

½ cup dry white wine

½ cup chopped fresh parsley

¼ cup all-purpose flour

1 teaspoon salt

1 teaspoon red pepper flakes

Pinch of black pepper

1 cup Italian-style dry breadcrumbs

Directions

1. Preheat the oven to 350°F.

2. Peel shrimp and place in a strainer. Rinse shrimp under cold running water and transfer to a large mixing bowl. Place the scallops in a strainer, rinse in the same manner, and add to the shrimp.

3. In a separate bowl, place the garlic, melted butter, heavy cream, cheeses, wine, parsley, flour, and salt, and whisk thoroughly to combine well.

4. Place the shrimp and scallops in a large cast-iron gratin dish or a similar baking dish. Pour the cheese mixture over the seafood and toss to thoroughly combine. Sprinkle evenly with the red pepper flakes and black pepper, then add an even layer of the breadcrumbs on top.

5. Bake for 20–25 minutes and serve.

"This is another dish I created to enhance our family's Christmas Eve dinner experience. I like to serve this dish over a simple white rice."

—FRANK

Chapter Six

DESSERTS

(DOLCI)

UNA LIRA FOR A WATERMELON

Watermelon—with its crisp, fleshy texture and slightly sweet taste that lingers on the tongue for just a little bit—has always been a favorite food of mine. After a long day working in the fields of my village, there was nothing quite as refreshing as a thick slice. But watermelon was a luxury, and not something we could have every day. This particular delectable was saved for special occasions. My father always liked to surprise us with something special when he went into the city to trade, and if he had any money left over, he would buy watermelon for me. So, as I was preparing to board the SS *Independence* and head to America for the first time, my mother stopped me on the docks to hand me something. I looked in my hand: una lira. Use it, she told me, to buy yourself some watermelon on the way to America.

I often replay this scene in my head because it captures so much about my mother. She did not want me to leave the small town she had come to adopt as her home, much less emigrate to America. She never said as much, but the idea that I would be living an ocean away pained her, especially as I was her only surviving daughter and my brothers, Vincenzo and Joe, had already moved away. And yet, there she stood, handing me money that must have required great sacrifice to save, so that I could purchase a treat on the voyage she did not want me to take.

My mother was born in Camden, New Jersey, in 1909, where she lived for only three years until work for Italians became scarce and the family had to move back to Italy. This is how my mother, and subsequently, I, came to be American citizens, though it was never something either of us really wanted. Like my mother, I had grown accustomed to small-town life. However, also like my mother, I had fallen in love with a man who would wind up taking me away from all that I knew.

165

LEMON AND YOGURT BUNDT CAKE

(Ciambellone allo Yogurt con Limone)

Serves 6–8 people

Ingredients

2½ cups all-purpose flour

2 teaspoons baking powder

Pinch of salt

1 cup unsalted butter, softened

1½ cups sugar

Zest and juice of 1 lemon

4 large eggs

½ cup vegetable oil

1 cup lemon yogurt or plain yogurt,
at room temperature

Confectioners' sugar, for garnish

For the glaze:

½ cup lemon juice

½ cup sugar

Directions

1. Preheat the oven to 350°F and grease a standard 10-inch Bundt pan with butter or oil.

2. Combine the flour, baking powder, and salt in a small bowl, and set aside. Using an electric stand mixer, fitted with a beater attachment, cream the butter, sugar, and lemon zest and juice, then add the eggs, one at a time, until incorporated. Reduce speed and add the flour mixture, oil, and ¼ cup of water, mixing until blended. Add the yogurt and mix thoroughly.

3. Pour the batter into the prepared Bundt pan and bake for 30–35 minutes. (The cake is ready when a toothpick inserted in the center of the cake comes out clean.) Remove the cake from the oven and let it cool in the pan on a wire rack for 10 minutes. Invert a plate or wire rack on top of the Bundt pan, then turn over gently, and remove the pan. Allow the cake to cool slightly.

4. *Prepare the glaze while the cake cools:* Heat the lemon juice and sugar in a small saucepan over medium heat, stirring until the sugar is dissolved. Pour the glaze on the warm cake. Allow the cake to cool completely, then garnish with confectioners' sugar.

NOTE

*For a thicker glaze, add the confectioners' sugar to the lemon
and juice in the saucepan.*

FRIED MILK BARS

(Fritti di Latte)

Ingredients

2 cups flour, plus 2 more cups for coating

1 cup sugar

4 cups whole milk

1 envelope of plain gelatin

1½ cinnamon sticks

Zest of 1 lemon, removed in strips

1 cup vegetable oil or peanut oil, for frying

4 eggs

Confectioners' sugar, crushed pecans, and ground cinnamon, for garnish (optional)

Directions

1. In a large bowl, mix 2 cups of flour and the sugar with a wooden spoon until combined, then slowly add the milk, stirring until mixed thoroughly. Transfer the mixture to a saucepan, add gelatin and heat over medium-low heat until the sugar is dissolved. Add the cinnamon sticks and lemon zest, and cook the mixture, stirring constantly, for 10 minutes, until silky. Remove the lemon zest and cinnamon stick.

2. Take enough parchment paper to line a 10 x 6-inch baking pan (or any similar-size pan), run the paper under cold running water, then fit the paper into the pan. Pour the mixture into the prepared baking pan and form into a 1-inch-thick rectangle, using an offset spatula or a rubber spatula to spread the mixture evenly. Refrigerate for 3–4 hours, or overnight.

3. Remove pan from the refrigerator. Turn the pan over onto a clean cutting board and peel away the paper. Cut the dough, with a long side facing you, into 4 horizontal rows and then 6 vertical rows, to create 24 small rectangles. (Or make smaller or larger pieces, if you like.)

4. Heat the oil in a nonstick frying pan. Beat the eggs in a small bowl. Place 2 cups of flour in another small bowl. Working with one rectangle at a time, dip each piece first into the flour, then eggs to coat, and then back into the flour to lightly coat, and transfer to a plate. Coat the remaining pieces in the same way. Fry 3–4 pieces at a time (do not the overcrowd pan) for about 2 minutes on each side, until lightly golden (do not fry too long). Transfer, as fried, to a wire rack. Serve warm, and garnish with a dusting of confectioners' sugar, pecans, or cinnamon, if desired.

THE HISTORY OF *FRITTI DI LATTE*

Fritti di Latte has a long history, dating back to Roman times. Different regions throughout Italy have developed their own version of this simple treat—some choose to add honey, while others add cocoa powder, or even breadcrumbs, to the outer crust. But the Abruzzo region, always committed to honoring true flavor and tradition, continues to prepare this amazing dessert using simple ingredients.

These treats were traditionally served during celebrations, especially in the autumn. However, for those who had access to fresh milk from their cows, they were served for breakfast with coffee, too. I often prepare them with the leftover cream from making my Italian rum cake or cream puffs (featured in my previous book, *Italian Moms: Spreading Their Art to Every Table*).

RICOTTA AND PEACHES

(Sformato di Ricotta con le Pesche)

Ingredients

2 cups fresh Ricotta cheese, drained well

½ cup sugar

Grated zest from 1 orange

1 teaspoon vanilla extract

4 tablespoons finely chopped fresh mint

3 tablespoons honey

1 packet of gelatin

4–6 fresh peaches (depending on size), peeled and sliced

1 cup apricot nectar juice

Fresh mint sprigs, for garnish

Directions

1. Combine the Ricotta, sugar, orange zest, vanilla extract, mint, and honey in a small bowl, and mix thoroughly. Heat the gelatin and ¼ cup of water for 3–4 minutes and add to the Ricotta mixture; blend thoroughly. Refrigerate the Ricotta mixture, covered with plastic wrap, for 1 hour, until chilled. Place the sliced peaches in a glass bowl and pour the apricot juice over the peaches. Refrigerate the peaches, covered with plastic wrap, until ready to serve the dessert.

2. *Form the Ricotta mixture into individual servings:* Remove the chilled cheese mixture from the refrigerator. Using a ½ cup measuring cup, scoop up the cheese mixture and press it down firmly to fill and pack the measuring cup. Turn over on a serving plate and place in the freezer for 30 minutes. Form more Ricotta cups in the same way.

3. To serve, remove the Ricotta from the freezer and spoon the marinated peaches on top. Garnish with a nice sprig of mint leaves.

NOTES

If you are running short on time, you can spoon the unchilled Ricotta mixture onto a plate and garnish with peaches, serving the dessert as a pudding, as was done before we had refrigerators. In the winter, you can also serve this as a warm dessert. Add 1 egg and 3 tablespoons of flour to the Ricotta mixture to make a batter. Preheat your oven to 350°F and grease 4 cups of a muffin tin. Evenly fill the cups with the batter and bake for 20–25 minutes. While the Ricotta is baking, heat your peaches with about ¼ cup apricot nectar juice in a small saucepan over low heat. When the Ricotta is baked, remove the Ricotta from the pan and place on individual plates. Top with your warm peaches and serve.

"This dessert is traditionally served in the month of August during the Ferragosto, the two-week period when all of Italy takes time off from work to celebrate religious holidays and visit relatives. (Perhaps the origin of this holiday has something to do with the August heat and the lack of air-conditioning in earlier times.) If peaches are not in season when you'd like to create this crowd pleaser, you can use peach preserves or jarred, marinated peaches. A chilled espresso latte makes a perfect pairing."

—ELISA

RICOTTA FANS

(Sfogliatelle)

(*Please note:* This recipe is for an experienced baker.)

Ingredients

For the dough:

2½ cups flour, plus more if necessary to smooth the dough

1 teaspoon salt

For the filling:

¼ cup sugar

½ cup semolina flour

16 ounces Ricotta cheese, well drained

2 large eggs

2 teaspoons vanilla extract

Pinch of ground cinnamon

Zest of 2 oranges

¾ cup solid shortening

½ cup unsalted butter

Confectioners' sugar, for garnish

Directions

1. In a bowl, combine the flour and salt. Turn out onto a clean wooden or marble-like surface to create a mound, then create a well in the center. Add ¾ cup of cold water to the center of the well and, gradually, using your hands, incorporate the flour into the water to create a dough. Knead the dough for 10–15 minutes. Form the dough into a ball and wrap it in plastic wrap. Refrigerate the dough for about 2 hours.

2. While the dough is chilling, *prepare the filling:* Bring the sugar and 1 cup of water to a boil in a medium saucepan over medium heat, stirring until the sugar is dissolved. Reduce heat to low, add the semolina in a stream, and cook, stirring occasionally, until the mixture begins to bubble.

3. Fold the Ricotta cheese into the mixture and cook for 2–3 minutes more. Remove from the heat and add the eggs, vanilla extract, cinnamon, and orange zest, whisking in the saucepan until you have a creamy consistency. Place plastic wrap directly on top of the cream, pressing down on the cream, and refrigerate until ready to use.

4. When the dough is chilled, remove it from refrigerator and flatten with a rolling pin into a strip still wide enough to pass through a pasta machine. Pass the dough through your pasta machine twice on the widest setting. Fold the dough in half and pass it through two more times. Repeat this process 2 dozen more times until the dough is silky.

5. If the texture is still coarse, sprinkle some flour on the dough and pass the dough through the machine until the dough is silky. Once again, form the dough into a ball and refrigerate, covered in plastic, for 1 hour.

6. While the dough is chilling, beat the shortening and butter with an electric stand mixer on high speed until light and fluffy.

7. When the dough is chilled, remove from the refrigerator and cut into 3 equal-sized pieces. Pass each piece through your pasta machine, adjusting the setting after each pass until you have passed the dough through the thinnest setting twice.

8. Cut the strips of dough into 12-inch-long pieces and brush with the shortening mixture.

9. Preheat the oven to 350°F and line two baking sheets with greased parchment paper.

10. Beginning with a short end of one piece of dough, start rolling the dough into a cylinder shape. Place on top of another dough piece and continue to roll. Repeat this until you have about five layers in the cylinder. Trim edges, wrap cylinder in plastic wrap, and place in the freezer for 15–20 minutes. Make two more rolls in the same way.

11. Remove your rolls from the freezer and slice into ½-inch disks. Working with one disk at a time, pick the dough up and cradle, a cut side down, in the fingers of both hands. Working from the middle of the disk outward, spin the disk in your fingers, pushing the middle out to form a cone. Fill the cone with 1 teaspoon of the Ricotta cream and seal the edge firmly with your fingers. Lay the *sfogliatelle* on the prepared baking sheets and brush the tops liberally with the remaining shortening mixture. Bake for 20–25 minutes, until golden brown. Remove from the oven and cool on wire racks. Dust with confectioners' sugar before serving.

CHOCOLATE CHRISTMAS COOKIES

(Scarponi di Natale Abruzzesi)

Ingredients

1 cup semisweet chocolate chips

1 cup sugar

2 tablespoons solid shortening

4 cups all-purpose flour

1 tablespoon baking powder

1 tablespoon cinnamon

2 large eggs

1 cup cooking wine

1 teaspoon Sambuca

¼ cup vegetable oil

Zest of 1 orange

¼ cup chopped dried
mandarin oranges

½ cup white raisins

1½ cups slivered almonds

1½ cups chopped walnuts

1½ cups chopped hazelnuts

1½ cups chopped
macadamia nuts

Directions

1. Preheat the oven to 400°F and line two baking sheets with parchment paper.

2. In a small saucepan, melt the chocolate chips, sugar, and solid shortening over medium heat, stirring constantly, until smooth. Remove from heat and set aside. In a large mixing bowl, combine the flour, baking powder, and cinnamon. In a separate bowl, beat the eggs, cooking wine, Sambuca, and vegetable oil with an electric stand mixer, fitted with a beater attachment, until combined. Reduce speed to low and slowly add the flour mixture to the egg mixture. Fold in the chocolate mixture and knead by hand until a thick dough forms. Add the orange zest, dried mandarin oranges, and raisins, and fold into the dough. Finally, add the nuts and fold into the dough.

3. Drop mounds of dough, each a generous tablespoon, 2 inches apart, onto the lined baking sheets and bake for 20–25 minutes, until the ends brown. Remove and cool on wire racks.

PLUM CAKES

Ingredients

3 large eggs

1 cup sugar

Pinch of salt

4 tablespoons unsalted butter, melted,
plus more for greasing the pan

2 tablespoons vanilla sugar

1 cup apricot yogurt

3 tablespoons whole milk

2 cups self-rising flour

½ cup vegetable oil

¼ cup of chocolate chips (optional)

Directions

1. Preheat the oven to 325°F. Grease the twelve rectangular cups of a mini bread loaf pan or one regular size loaf pan with butter.

2. With an electric stand mixer, fitted with a beater attachment, beat the eggs, sugar, and salt until creamy. Add the melted butter and vanilla sugar, and beat until light and fluffy. Add the yogurt and milk, a few tablespoons at a time, then slowly add the flour and continue to beat until thoroughly blended. Finally, add the oil in a stream and beat until incorporated. If using the chocolate chips, fold them into the batter.

3. If using mini loaf pans, fill each prepared pan three-fourths full; if using a regular-size pan, use all batter to fill the prepared pan. Bake the mini cakes for 30–35 minutes; add 10–15 minutes for the regular-size loaf. Do not open the oven before the minimum cooking time; the cakes are done when a toothpick inserted in the center of the cake comes out clean. Remove pans and carefully turn over cakes onto wire racks to cool.

PANNA COTTA

Ingredients

2 cups whipping cream

½ cup sugar

1 tablespoon vanilla extract

1½ tablespoons plain gelatin powder

Berries, caramel sauce, or chocolate
sauce, for garnish

Directions

1. In a medium saucepan, combine the cream, sugar, and vanilla extract, whisking constantly. Bring to a boil over medium heat, and boil for 2 minutes. Remove pan from the heat and whisk the gelatin powder into the mixture, whisking until thoroughly combined. Pour mixture into a measuring cup with a spout, then pour into nonstick *panna cotta* molds or dessert molds. Refrigerate, covered with plastic wrap, for at least 3 hours before serving.

2. To serve, remove *panna cotta* molds from the refrigerator and place in a pot. Carefully add about 2 inches of hot water to the pot (avoid getting water in the molds). Working with one mold at a time, remove mold from the water, invert an individual serving plate over each mold, and turn over the plate and the mold to unmold the *panna cotta*. Unmold the remaining *panna cottas* in the same way. Garnish each one with berries, caramel sauce, or chocolate sauce, and serve.

ALMOND, LEMON, AND RICOTTA CAKE

(Torta di Ricotta, Mandorla e Limone)

Serves 8–10 people

Ingredients

Unsalted butter for greasing
the pan

1½ cups slivered almonds

½ cup sugar

1 teaspoon baking powder

¼ teaspoon salt

3 large eggs, separated

1¾ cups Ricotta cheese, drained

Zest of 2 lemons

Juice of 1 lemon

1 tablespoon vanilla extract

Directions

1. Preheat the oven to 350°F and grease a 9-inch springform pan with butter or oil.

2. Using a blender or a food processor, grind the almonds. In a large mixing bowl, combine the ground almonds, sugar, baking powder, and salt. In a separate mixing bowl, combine the egg yolks, Ricotta, lemon zest, lemon juice, and vanilla extract, and whisk until thoroughly blended. Add the Ricotta mixture to the almond mixture and blend together.

3. In a small bowl, whisk the egg whites until foamy and fold into the batter.

4. Pour the batter into the prepared springform pan and bake for 50–55 minutes, until golden and the center of the cake is cooked. (The cake is done when a toothpick inserted in the center of the cake comes out clean.)

5. Allow the cake to cool completely in the pan on a wire rack, then refrigerate, covered with plastic wrap, for at least 3 hours before serving. To serve, remove the cake from the springform pan, and transfer to a cake plate.

ANISETTE BISCOTTI

(Biscotti all'Anice)

Ingredients

8 tablespoons salted butter

1¼ cups sugar

2 eggs

2 cups all-purpose flour, plus
more for dusting

1½ teaspoons baking powder

½ teaspoon salt

1 teaspoon vanilla extract

3 teaspoons anisette seeds

Directions

1. Preheat the oven to 350°F and line two baking sheets with parchment paper.

2. With a handheld mixer or an electric stand mixer on medium speed, cream the butter, sugar, and eggs. Reduce speed to low, then add the flour, baking powder, salt, vanilla extract, and anisette seeds, and mix until the dough is thoroughly blended.

3. Dust a clean work surface with flour and divide the dough into four equal-sized parts. (For larger biscotti, you can divide the dough into 3 equal-sized parts.) Roll out each piece into a log about 2 inches wide. Place two logs, 2–3 inches apart, on each of the lined baking sheets and bake for 30 minutes. Remove from oven and let cool.

NOTE

I tend not to toast the biscotti, but if you like, once the logs cool, slice logs into ½-inch-thick pieces, place the biscotti back on the baking sheet, cut sides down, and toast for 5–10 minutes. Remove from the oven and cool on wire racks.

POLENTA POUND CAKE

(Torta di Polenta)

Ingredients

16 tablespoons unsalted butter, softened, plus more for greasing the pan

1 cup sugar

Zest of 1 lemon

3 eggs

2 teaspoons vanilla extract

½ cup plain yogurt

½ cup polenta corn flour

1 cup all-purpose flour

½ teaspoon baking powder

Pinch of salt

Confectioners' sugar, for garnish

Directions

1. Preheat the oven to 350°F and grease an 8 x 5-inch loaf pan with butter or oil.

2. With an electric stand mixer or a handheld electric mixer on medium speed, cream the butter, sugar, and lemon zest until blended and fluffy. Add the eggs, one at a time, beating until each egg is thoroughly blended into the butter mixture. Reduce speed to low, and add the vanilla extract and yogurt. Finally, add the polenta flour, the all-purpose flour, baking powder, and salt, beating until the batter is a uniform consistency and smooth.

3. Spoon the batter into the prepared loaf pan and bake for 1 hour, or until golden brown. (The cake is done when a toothpick inserted in the center of the cake comes out clean.) Remove from the oven and allow the cake to cool in the pan for 10 minutes. Turn the cake over onto a wire rack and allow it to cool completely. Before serving, garnish the top of the cake with a sprinkle of confectioners' sugar.

AMARETTO PARFAIT

(Dolce Semifreddo Agli Amaretti)

Ingredients

For the cookies:

3 large eggs, separated

1¼ cups granulated sugar,
plus 1 tablespoon

4 cups almond meal flour

1 teaspoon lemon juice

1 cup confectioners' sugar

For the cake:

Salted butter, for greasing the pans

1 box butter cake mix with pudding

4 eggs

½ cup vegetable oil

1 cup whole milk

1 shot amaretto liqueur

For the cream:

6 egg yolks

12 tablespoons sugar

6 tablespoons all-purpose flour

3½ cups whole milk

1 (3-inch) cinnamon stick

Whole peel of half a lemon

For the assembly:

3 pounds mixed berries

8 tablespoons salted butter

½ cup amaretto liqueur

¾ cup confectioners' sugar

Directions

1. *Prepare the cookies:* Using an electric stand mixer, fitted with a whisk attachment, whisk the egg yolks, then gradually add 1¼ cups of sugar, whisking until well blended. Add the almond flour and whisk at low speed (do not overmix). In a separate bowl, beat the egg whites on high speed until soft peaks form. Using a large rubber spatula, fold one-third of the egg whites into the almond mixture. Add the lemon juice and the remaining egg whites and blend with the spatula until a dough forms. Refrigerate the amaretto cookie dough, covered with plastic wrap, for at least 1 hour, or overnight.

2. Preheat the oven to 325°F and line two baking sheets with parchment paper.

3. Roll the amaretto dough into balls the size of small walnuts. Place confectioners' sugar in a bowl. Coat the balls in confectioners' sugar and place twenty balls on each lined baking sheet. Bake until lightly golden, about 25–30 minutes. Remove from the oven and cool cookies on a wire rack.

4. Preheat the oven to 350°F and grease and salt two 9-inch cake pans.

5. *Prepare the cake:* Place the cake mix in the mixing bowl of an electric stand mixer, fitted with a beater attachment. With the mixer on low, add the eggs and beat until combined. Add the oil, milk, and amaretto, and beat for 5 minutes until mixed thoroughly. Divide batter evenly between the prepared baking pans and bake for 45–60 minutes, until the top is lightly browned and the center is baked. (The cake is done when a toothpick inserted in the center of the cake comes out clean.). Immediately remove the cake from the pans and set on a wire rack to cool completely.

6. *Prepare the cream:* Using an electric stand mixer, fitted with a beater attachment, beat the egg yolks and sugar on medium speed for 15 minutes. Reduce speed to low, and slowly add the flour, beating until combined. Add the milk and beat until blended thoroughly.

7. Pour the mixture into a medium saucepan. Add the cinnamon stick and lemon peel and bring to a boil over medium heat, stirring constantly. As soon as the first bubbles appear, remove from the heat and transfer to a glass bowl. Remove the cinnamon stick and the lemon peel. Place wax paper directly on top of the cream to prevent a film from forming and refrigerate for at least 1 hour.

8. *Assemble the parfait in one large glass bowl or in individual parfait dessert cups:* Whether you are using a parfait bowl or dessert cups, the assembly is the same. Slice each cake layer horizontally to create four layers. If you are using one large glass parfait bowl and it is less than 9 inches in diameter, turn the bowl over and use it as a cookie cutter to cut the cakes into rounds to fit your bowl. If you are using dessert cups, you can either use one of the cups as a cutter to cut the cake into rounds to fit your container or you can crumble the cakes into a bowl and create cake layers with the crumbled cake. If you're stamping out the rounds, you will need three rounds per container.

9. Place a layer of cake in the parfait bowl or dessert cups. Add a layer of cream and then top with a layer of the berries. (You can mix the berries all together, or use one type per layer, whichever you prefer.) Continue to layer with cake, cream, and berries, and then repeat one more time. Add the remaining cream and then arrange some of your amaretto cookies on top.

10. *Prepare the icing:* Heat the butter, amaretto, and sugar in a saucepan over low heat, stirring, then bring to a simmer, stirring occasionally, and cook until the icing reaches the correct consistency.

11. Drizzle the icing on top of the cookies. Place the parfait or parfaits in the refrigerator and serve within 2–3 hours.

"Here is another example of taking something old and giving it a modern twist. This fresh new dessert is actually a combination of Mom's whiskey cake recipe, her amaretto cookies, and a classic cream. You can prepare this in a large parfait bowl or in individual dessert cups."

—FRANK

3. *Prepare the traditional cream:* Using an electric stand mixer, fitted with a beater attachment, beat the egg yolks and sugar on medium speed for 15 minutes. Reduce speed to low, and slowly add the flour, beating until combined. Add the milk and beat until blended thoroughly. Pour the mixture into a medium saucepan. Add the cinnamon stick and the lemon peel and bring to a boil over medium heat, stirring constantly. As soon as the first bubbles appear, remove from the heat and transfer to a glass bowl. Remove the cinnamon stick and the lemon peel. Place wax paper directly on top of the cream filling to prevent a film from forming, and refrigerate for at least 1 hour.

4. *Prepare the chocolate cream:* Repeat the process of making the traditional cream (step 3). After removing the cinnamon and lemon peel, stir in the 12-ounce bag of unsweetened chocolate chips. Continue to stir until all the chips have melted. Place wax paper directly on top of the chocolate cream filling to prevent a film from forming and refrigerate for at least 1 hour.

5. *Prepare the whipped cream topping just before assembling the trifle:* With an electric stand mixer, fitted with a beater attachment, beat the heavy cream at high speed and gradually add the sugar and vanilla extract. Continue to beat until light and fluffy (approximately 5–7 minutes for the entire step).

6. *Assemble the trifle:* Slice off the tops of the cakes to form flat tops. Slice the cakes horizontally in half to create four equal layers (you will only use three of these cake layers in the trifle). In a 9-inch trifle bowl, place the first layer of cake in the bottom of the bowl and press firmly. Brush the cake with some rum and add half of the traditional cream to the bowl in a single layer. Sprinkle the cream with some nuts. Add the next layer of cake, brush with some rum, and then a layer of half the chocolate cream. Sprinkle with some nuts.

7. Repeat layering another entire set of layers, following the same process as above. Finish the trifle by adding a layer of the whipped cream topping. Garnish with the remaining nuts and the chocolate chips and refrigerate, covered with plastic wrap, until ready to serve.

ITALIAN LEMON KNOT COOKIES

(Tarallucci al Limone)

Makes 4 dozen cookies

Ingredients

For the cookies:

4 large eggs

1 cup sugar

¾ cup vegetable oil

½ cup heavy cream

Zest and juice of 1 lemon

4 cups all-purpose flour,
plus more for dusting

4 teaspoons baking powder

For the glaze:

1½ cups confectioners' sugar

5 tablespoons heavy cream

1 lemon juice

Candy sprinkles, for garnish

Directions

1. *Prepare the cookie dough:* Using an electric stand mixer, fitted with a whisk attachment, whisk the eggs and sugar on medium speed until light and fluffy. Reduce speed to low, then add the oil, heavy cream, lemon zest, and lemon juice, and blend thoroughly. Slowly sift in the flour and baking powder, and mix until well blended. Transfer the dough to another bowl and refrigerate, covered with plastic wrap, for 2 hours.

2. Preheat the oven to 350°F and line two (or however many you need) baking sheets with parchment paper.

3. Remove the dough from the refrigerator. Dust a clean work surface heavily with some flour. Scoop 1 tablespoon of dough and drop onto the floured surface. Using the tips of your fingers, roll the dough into a log approximately 4 inches long. Form a horseshoe shape with the strip of dough and twist the ends twice to form a knot. Place the knot on a parchment-lined baking sheet. Make more cookies in the same manner with the remaining dough and place on baking sheets, leaving 1–2 inches between each knot.

4. Bake for 10–12 minutes, until the edges are lightly brown. Remove from the oven and cool on wire racks.

5. When the knots are cool, *prepare the glaze:* In a small saucepan, combine the confectioners' sugar, heavy cream, and lemon juice over low heat, and whisk until blended thoroughly. Remove from the heat. Using a pastry brush, brush the glaze on top of the knots, then add sprinkles.

SWEET TARALLI

(Taralli Dolci di Pasqua)

Makes 2 dozen taralli

Ingredients

For the dough:

6 cups flour, plus more for dusting

1½ tablespoons baking powder

6 eggs

½ cup sugar

½ cup light brown sugar

¼ cup vegetable oil

⅔ cup butter, melted

2 teaspoons vanilla

For the glaze:

3 cups confectioners' sugar

4 tablespoons water

2 teaspoons lemon juice

1 teaspoon vanilla

Rainbow sprinkles or silver balls sprinkles, for garnish

Directions

1. Preheat the oven to 350°F and line two baking sheets with parchment paper.

2. *Prepare the dough:* In a large bowl, mix together the flour and baking powder. Pour the flour mixture onto a clean wooden or marble-like surface in a mound and form a well in the center of the flour. In a separate mixing bowl, combine the eggs, sugars, oil, butter, and vanilla, and whisk together. Pour the egg mixture into the well. Using your hands, fold the flour into the egg mixture until a dough is formed. Place the dough in a lightly floured bowl, cover with a kitchen towel, and set aside for 20 minutes.

3. Turn out the dough onto a lightly floured surface and knead the dough for 3–4 minutes. Divide the dough into four equal-sized pieces. Using the palms of your hands, roll each piece of dough into a rope (similar to making gnocchi). Cut the rope of dough into 2-inch pieces. Form each piece of dough into a circle and pinch the ends together to secure the circle. Place the taralli on the parchment-lined baking sheets 1 inch apart and bake for 30–35 minutes, until lightly golden. Remove and place on a wire rack to cool.

4. *Prepare the glaze and finish the cookies:* In a small saucepan, combine all the glaze ingredients (except the sprinkles) and heat over medium heat, stirring until thoroughly blended. Remove glaze from the heat and let cool for 5 minutes. Using a pastry brush, brush the glaze on the top of the cookies. Top with the sprinkles.

WHITE CHOCOLATE MACADAMIA NUT BISCOTTI

(Biscotti alle Mocciole con Cioccolato Bianco)

Ingredients

1 cup macadamia nuts

2 eggs

8 tablespoons salted butter, softened

1½ cups sugar

2 cups all-purpose flour, sifted, plus more for dusting

1½ teaspoons baking powder

1 teaspoon vanilla extract

1 cup white chocolate chips

NOTES

For crispy biscotti, you can return the cut logs to the oven and bake for 5–10 minutes more, then cool on wire racks. For a fancy presentation, melt some additional white chocolate chips with some solid shortening, then drizzle over the biscotti, and top with some toasted nuts.

Directions

1. Preheat the oven to 350°F and line two baking sheets with parchment paper.

2. Scatter macadamia nuts evenly on a baking sheet and roast in the oven for about 20 minutes. Stir the nuts occasionally with a wooden spoon for even browning. Remove the roasted nuts from the oven and allow them to cool. Chop nuts and set aside.

3. With an electric stand mixer, fitted with a beater attachment, cream the eggs, butter, and sugar on medium speed. Reduce the speed to low, then add the flour, baking powder, vanilla extract, white chocolate chips, and the chopped roasted nuts, and beat until all the ingredients are mixed thoroughly.

4. Lightly flour a clean work surface and divide the dough into four equal-sized parts. With a rolling pin, roll out each piece into a log about 2 inches wide. Place two logs, side by side and 2–3 inches apart, on each of the lined baking sheets and bake for 30 minutes. Remove from the oven and transfer the logs to a cutting board. Cut the logs into 1-inch-diagonal strips and allow biscotti to cool on wire racks.

LEMON POPPY BISCOTTI

(Biscotti al Limone e Semi di Papavero)

Ingredients

2 eggs

8 tablespoons salted butter, softened

1 ½ cups sugar

2 cups all-purpose flour, sifted, plus
more for dusting

1 ½ teaspoons baking powder

1 tablespoon lemon extract

1 tablespoon lemon rind

¾ cup poppy seeds, plus more
for the glaze

Juice of 1 lemon

¼ cup solid shortening

1 cup confectioners' sugar

Directions

1. Preheat the oven to 350°F and line two baking sheets with parchment paper.

2. With an electric stand mixer, fitted with a beater attachment, cream the eggs, butter, and sugar on medium speed. Reduce the speed to low, then add the flour, baking powder, lemon extract, and lemon rind, and blend until mixed thoroughly. Finally, add the poppy seeds and fold in thoroughly.

3. Lightly flour a clean work surface and divide the dough into four equal-sized parts. With a rolling pin, roll out each piece into a log about 2 inches wide. Place two logs, side by side and 2–3 inches apart, on each of the lined baking sheets and bake for 30 minutes. Remove from the oven and transfer the logs to a cutting board. Cut the logs into 1-inch-diagonal strips and allow biscotti to cool on wire racks.

4. In a small saucepan, combine the lemon juice, solid shortening, and confectioners' sugar, and stir constantly over low heat until combined well. Remove from the heat and cool for a few minutes. Add some poppy seeds and mix thoroughly. Drizzle glaze on top of the biscotti.

NOTE

For crispy biscotti, at the end of step 3 you can return the cut logs to the oven and bake for 5–10 minutes more, then cool on wire racks.

BUTTERSCOTCH BISCOTTI

(Biscotti al Butterscotch)

Ingredients

2 eggs

8 tablespoons salted butter, softened

1½ cups sugar

2 cups all-purpose flour, sifted,
plus more for dusting

1½ teaspoons baking powder

1 teaspoon vanilla extract

2 cups butterscotch chips

Directions

1. Preheat the oven to 350°F.

2. With an electric stand mixer, fitted with a beater attachment, cream the eggs, butter, and sugar. Reduce the speed to low, then add the flour, baking powder, and vanilla extract, and beat until mixed thoroughly. Finally, add butterscotch chips to the batter and fold in thoroughly.

3. Lightly flour a clean work surface and divide the dough into four equal parts. With a rolling pin, roll out each piece into a log about 2 inches wide. Place two logs, side by side, and 2–3 inches apart, on each of the lined baking sheets and bake for 30 minutes. Remove from the oven and transfer the logs to a cutting board. Cut the logs into 1-inch-diagonal strips and allow biscotti to cool on wire racks.

NOTE

For crispy biscotti, you can return the cut logs to the oven and bake for 5–10 minutes more, then cool on wire racks.

DEATH BY CHOCOLATE TRIFLE

(Semifreddo di Cioccolato Tartufato)

Serves 6–8 people

Ingredients

For the cake:

2 large eggs

1½ cups sugar

2 cups all-purpose flour

2 teaspoons baking powder

2 teaspoons baking soda

1 teaspoon vanilla extract

¾ cup cocoa powder

¾ cup vegetable oil

1 cup whole milk or heavy cream

1 cup hot espresso coffee

For the chocolate cream:

6 egg yolks

12 tablespoons sugar

6 tablespoons all-purpose flour

3 ½ cups whole milk

1 (3-inch) cinnamon stick

Whole peel of half a lemon

1 (12-ounce) bag unsweetened chocolate chips

For the frosting:

2 cups salted butter, softened

6 cups confectioners' sugar

½ cup cocoa powder

8 tablespoons whipping cream

¼ cup chocolate liqueur

4 teaspoons vanilla extract

Chocolate chips and/or chocolate shavings, for garnish

Directions

1. Preheat the oven to 350°F. Grease two 9-inch cake pans with oil.

2. *Prepare the cake:* With an electric stand mixer, fitted with a beater attachment, beat the eggs and sugar until creamy. Sift in the flour, baking powder, and baking soda, then add the vanilla extract, and beat for 5 minutes more.

3. Add the cocoa powder, oil, and milk and continue to beat for 5 minutes more. Finally, add the espresso coffee and beat for 2 minutes more. Pour the batter evenly into the two prepared pans and bake for 40–45 minutes. The cake is done when a toothpick inserted into the center comes out clean. Immediately remove cakes from the pans and set aside on a wire rack to cool completely.

4. *Prepare the chocolate cream:* With an electric stand mixer, fitted with a beater attachment, beat the egg yolks and sugar on medium speed for 15 minutes. Reduce speed to low, and slowly add the flour, beating until combined. Add the milk and beat until blended thoroughly. Pour the mixture into a medium saucepan. Add the cinnamon stick and lemon peel, and bring to a boil over medium heat, stirring constantly. As soon as the first bubbles appear, remove from the heat. Remove the cinnamon and lemon peel, then stir in the chocolate chips and continue to stir until all the chips have melted and the mixture is well combined. Transfer the chocolate cream to a glass bowl. Place wax paper directly on the surface to prevent a film from forming. Refrigerate at least 1 hour.

5. *Prepare the frosting:* With an electric stand mixer, fitted with a beater attachment, beat the butter on high speed until fluffy. Reduce the speed to medium, add the confectioners' sugar, and beat until well combined. Reduce speed to low, add the cocoa powder, whipping cream, chocolate liqueur, and vanilla extract, and blend until the mixture is smooth. Increase the speed to high, and beat until the frosting is fluffy (the entire step should take 5–7 minutes).

6. *Assemble the trifle:* Slice off the tops of the cake layers (reserving the tops) to form layers with flat tops. In a 9-inch trifle bowl, place 1 layer of cake in the bottom of the bowl. Using half of the chocolate cream, add a layer of cream to the bowl. Add the remaining layer of cake, and then a layer of the remaining cream. Using one of the tops you removed from the cakes, add it to the bowl to top the layer of cream. Finally, top the trifle with a layer of the frosting. Garnish with the chocolate chips and/or shavings and refrigerate until ready to serve.

NOTE

You can also use individual dessert cups for this decadent dessert. Simply crumble layers of the cake, press it firmly with your fingertips into your serving cups, and follow the layering process specified above.

"We have taken Mom's classic chocolate cake and chocolate cream,
and added a rich chocolate frosting to create a modern party dessert."

——FRANK

FLORENTINES

(Biscotti Fiorentini)

Makes 2 dozen cookies

Ingredients

4 tablespoons unsalted butter

³/₄ cup confectioners' sugar

½ cup all-purpose flour

3 tablespoons heavy cream

3 tablespoons honey

Zest and juice of 1 orange

1¼ cups slivered almonds,
finely chopped

For the chocolate topping:

3 teaspoons solid shortening

2 cups semi-sweet chocolate chips
or white chocolate chips

¼ cup slivered almonds, finely
chopped, for garnish

Directions

1. Preheat the oven to 350°F and line two baking sheets with parchment paper.

2. In a medium saucepan, melt the butter over low heat. Add the confectioners' sugar, flour, heavy cream, honey, and orange juice, and whisk until smooth and free of lumps. Increase heat to medium-high and bring to a boil, continuing to whisk until thickened. Remove pan from the heat and add the orange zest and almonds. Set the pan aside and allow the dough to cool for 10 minutes.

3. Drop 1 teaspoon measures of dough, 2 inches apart, onto the lined baking sheets, and bake for 15–20 minutes, until lightly brown. Remove from oven. Let cookies cool slightly, then transfer with a wooden or rubber spatula to a wire rack to cool completely.

4. *Prepare the chocolate topping:* In a medium saucepan, place the shortening and chocolate chips and stir over medium heat until melted. Pour the topping into a measuring cup with a pouring spout.

5. Place some parchment paper under the wire rack, and drizzle the warm chocolate topping over the cookies. Garnish tops with the almonds and allow topping to cool for 20 minutes before serving.

CHOCOLATE-COVERED ALMOND CAKE

(Parrozzo de Abruzzo)

Serves 8–10 people

Ingredients

For the cake:

1 cup all-purpose flour

¼ cup semolina flour

1 teaspoon baking powder

½ teaspoon salt

1 cup slivered almonds

6 tablespoons unsalted butter, softened

¾ cup sugar

5 large eggs

1 teaspoon almond extract

Zest of 1 lemon

For the glaze:

1½ cups semisweet chocolate chips

2 tablespoons unsalted butter

1 tablespoon amaretto liqueur

Slivered almonds, for garnish

Directions

1. *Prepare the cake:* Preheat the oven to 350°F and grease a 10-inch Bundt pan with butter or oil.

2. Place the flour, semolina, baking powder, and salt in a mixing bowl. Using a blender or food processor, grind the almonds to a powder. Add almond powder to the flour mixture and set aside. With an electric stand mixer, fitted with a beater attachment, cream the butter and sugar on medium speed until fluffy. Add the eggs, one at a time, beating until combined well, then add the almond extract and lemon zest, and beat until mixed thoroughly. Reduce speed to low, then slowly add the flour mixture, beating until thoroughly combined.

3. Pour the cake batter into the prepared Bundt pan and bake for 45–50 minutes, until a toothpick inserted in the center comes out clean. Cool the cake in the pan on a rack for 15 minutes. Invert onto a wire rack, and cool completely.

4. When the cake is cool, *prepare the glaze:* In a small saucepan, melt the chocolate chips over medium heat, then add the butter and amaretto liqueur, whisking until silky smooth. Remove from heat and pour the glaze into a measuring cup with a pouring spout.

5. Place the cake on a serving plate and pour the warm glaze on top in a back-and-forth motion, or any design you like. Allow the glaze to settle for a few minutes, then cover the top with slivered almonds. Allow the cake to cool completely before serving.

CHOCOLATE PANINI COOKIES

(Panini Dolci al Cioccolato)

Ingredients

For the cookies:

2 sticks unsalted butter, softened

¾ cup sugar

1 egg

1 teaspoon vanilla extract

1½ cups all-purpose flour

For the filling:

2 tablespoons unsalted butter

1½ cups semisweet chocolate chips

2 tablespoons coffee liqueur or chocolate liqueur

3 teaspoons light corn syrup or honey

Directions

1. Preheat the oven to 350°F and line two baking sheets with parchment paper.

2. *Prepare the cookies:* With an electric stand mixer, fitted with a beater attachment, cream the butter and sugar on low speed. Add the egg and vanilla extract, and increase the speed to blend thoroughly. Reduce the speed and gradually add the flour, blending until the dough has a creamy consistency. (The entire step should take approximately 5–7 minutes.)

3. Place the cookie dough in a pastry bag, fitted with a plain tip. Pipe 2-inch-long strips of dough, 2 inches apart, onto the lined baking sheets and bake for 10 minutes, until golden brown. Remove from the oven and cool the cookies on a wire rack.

4. *Prepare the filling:* In a medium saucepan, melt the butter and chocolate chips over low heat, stirring constantly with a wooden spoon to keep from burning the chocolate. Gradually add the liqueur and corn syrup, and blend thoroughly. Remove from the heat and prepare your panini while the filling is still warm.

5. Assemble the paninis: Turn over half the cookies, flat sides facing up, and spread chocolate filling over the flat sides of these cookies. Sandwich each chocolate-topped cookie with a plain cookie to form a panini.

CELEBRATING SAN GIUSEPPE

As you have seen, many of my dishes figure prominently in a particular celebration or holiday. Growing up, the food we had on our table greatly depended on the resources available and the traditions handed down by our ancestors. The feast day of San Giuseppe—St. Joseph—is no different.

Celebrated on March 19, the celebration of St. Joseph dates back to the middle ages. St. Joseph, the mortal father of Jesus, is accredited with answering the prayers of many Italians in southern Italy who were facing severe droughts. Italians believe that it was St. Joseph who brought the rain and ended the terrible droughts that left so many without food.

After the rain came, Italians thanked St. Joseph by bringing their first harvest to the feet of his statues throughout the churches in Italy. Today, following a nine-day prayer ritual, this tradition is still carried out. Some of the traditional harvest offerings include fava beans (during the droughts, they continued to grow, and many families survived on this bean, traditionally used to feed the livestock), chickpeas, fennel, bread, and citrus fruits.

As is the tradition on any religious holiday, Italians abstain from eating meat during the feast. Most tables are graced with a dish in St. Joseph's honor that consists of beans, sardines, thick pasta, and breadcrumbs (symbolizing the sawdust of St. Joseph, the carpenter). My family's version of this dish is shared in the pasta section of this book (St. Joseph's Day Pasta, page 80).

Many other traditions surround this important day. For example, family members with the name of Joseph or Josephine are allowed to sit at the head of the table, and they are given gifts. Even a tug on their earlobes is said to bring good luck. Traditional desserts used to celebrate the day are *Calzone di San Giuseppe* and *Zeppole di San Giuseppe*.

ST. JOSEPH CALZONE COOKIES

(Calzone di San Giuseppe)

Makes 4–5 dozen cookies

Ingredients

For the filling:

4 cups canned chickpeas, drained

3 tablespoons dark brown sugar

3 tablespoons granulated sugar

4 tablespoons honey

1 tablespoon fresh lemon juice

Zest of 1 lemon

1 teaspoon vanilla extract

1 teaspoon nutmeg

1 teaspoon ground cinnamon

For the dough:

1 cup granulated sugar

1 cup whole milk

3 large eggs

¾ cup vegetable oil

2 teaspoons vanilla extract

5 cups all-purpose flour, plus more for dusting

About 4 cups vegetable oil, for frying

Confectioners' sugar, for garnish

Directions

1. *Prepare the filling:* Using a blender or food processor, grind the chickpeas, 1 cup at a time, and place them in a large glass mixing bowl. Add the remaining filling ingredients and stir until thoroughly combined and a smooth consistency. Refrigerate, covered with plastic wrap, while you prepare the dough.

2. *Prepare the dough:* In a large mixing bowl, combine the sugar, milk, eggs, oil, and vanilla, and whisk until well blended. Gradually stir in the flour until a dough forms. Turn the dough onto a clean floured work surface and knead the dough for 5–6 minutes.

3. Divide the dough into four equal-sized parts. Working with one piece of dough at a time, and using a rolling pin or a pasta machine, roll the dough into a strip about ⅛ inch thick. With a 3-inch biscuit cutter or drinking glass, cut out dough rounds. Continue to make more dough rounds with the remaining pieces of dough, then use the scraps of dough to form more dough rounds.

4. Remove the filling from the refrigerator and place 1 teaspoon of filling onto the center of each dough round. Fold the dough over the filling to form a half-moon shape (similar to preparing ravioli). Seal the ends of the dough with a fork. With a pastry or ravioli wheel cutter, cut around the edges to keep them from opening when frying.

5. Pour enough oil into a medium saucepan to reach a depth of 4 inches and heat over medium heat for 5–7 minutes until oil is hot but not burning hot. Test the heat by placing one calzone in the oil and frying for 1–2 minutes. It should be golden brown on both sides. Adjust heat, if necessary. Remove the calzone with a slotted spoon and place it on a paper towel–lined wire rack to cool. Cook the remaining calzones in batches (do not overcrowd the pan) in the same way. Once cool, sift the confectioners' sugar over the calzones.

ST. JOSEPH CREAM PUFFS

(Zeppole di San Giuseppe)

Ingredients

For the pastry:

16 tablespoons salted butter, softened

2 tablespoons sugar

2 cups all-purpose flour

1 tablespoon baking powder

8 large eggs, at room temperature

For the cream filling:

2 egg yolks, at room temperature

½ cup sugar

2 tablespoons all-purpose flour

1 teaspoon vanilla extract

Zest of 1 orange

1 cinnamon stick

1 tablespoon rum

⅔ cup whole milk, at
room temperature

Confectioners' sugar, for garnish

Maraschino cherries, for garnish

Directions

1. Preheat the oven to 400°F and line a baking sheet with parchment paper.

2. *Prepare the pastry:* Place the butter, sugar, and 2 cups of water in a medium saucepan over medium heat, and bring to a full boil, whisking. Slowly add the flour and baking powder, whisking constantly, until the mixture forms a dough. Remove pan from the heat. Add one egg to the dough, whisking constantly, until mixed thoroughly, then continue to add and whisk in the remaining eggs, one at a time.

3. Place the dough in a piping bag fitted with a star tip. Pipe the dough into spiral forms (with a full base 3–4 inches wide and a dome two layers high) onto the lined baking sheet. Bake for 30 minutes, until puffed and light golden. Cool on a wire rack.

4. *Prepare the cream filling:* In a medium saucepan, combine the egg yolks, sugar, flour, vanilla extract, orange zest, cinnamon, and rum, and whisk over low heat until mixed thoroughly. Slowly add the milk, whisking until combined, then increase the heat to medium and continue to whisk for 3–4 minutes more. Remove pan from the heat and allow the cream to cool for 5–7 minutes to thicken.

5. With a serrated knife, gently cut off the tops of the puffs. Place cream in a piping bag and fill each puff with cream. Sift some confectioners' sugar over the puffs, and garnish with a dab of cream and a cherry. Refrigerate until ready to serve.

BUTTER COOKIES

(Biscotti al Burro)

Makes 3 dozen cookies

Ingredients

16 tablespoons unsalted butter,
softened

¾ cup sugar

1 egg

1 teaspoon vanilla extract

2½ cups all-purpose flour

1 teaspoon baking powder

Pinch of salt

Chocolate or rainbow sprinkles,
for decoration

Directions

1. Preheat the oven to 350°F and line three baking sheets with parchment paper.

2. With an electric stand mixer, fitted with a beater attachment, cream the butter and sugar on low speed. Add the egg and vanilla extract, and increase the speed to blend thoroughly. Reduce speed to low, and gradually add the flour, baking powder, and salt. Place the dough in a pastry bag, fitted with a star tip, or a cookie press.

3. Pipe 2-inch round disks of dough, about 2 inches apart, onto the lined baking sheets. Generously scatter sprinkles on the tops of the rounds and bake for 10–15 minutes, until golden brown. Remove from oven and cool cookies on a wire rack.

NOTE

You can make chocolate butter cookies by adding ½ cup of cocoa powder to the dough mixture.

ALMOND BARS

(Torrone di Natale alle Mandorle)

Ingredients

1 tablespoon solid shortening,
for greasing the baking sheet

4 cups whole almonds

4 cups sugar

1 cup water

1 lemon, halved

Directions

1. Preheat the oven to 350°F and grease a baking sheet with the shortening.

2. Place the almonds on another baking sheet and toast them in the oven, stirring and turning over occasionally, for 10 minutes.

3. In a saucepan, heat the sugar and 1 cup of water over low heat, stirring until the sugar is melted. Add the toasted almonds, increase the heat to medium, and cook the mixture, stirring, for 3–4 minutes. Pour the almonds and syrup onto the prepared baking sheet. Cover the almond mixture with wax paper, and using a rolling pin or a metal spatula, flatten the mixture to a ¼-inch thickness. Remove wax paper and rub the cut lemon halves across the top of the almond mixture, spreading the lemon evenly with your fingers. Slice into bars while still warm and allow to cool on wire racks.

FRESH BERRY RICE PUDDING PARFAITS

(Riso e Latte con Frutti di Bosco)

Serves 4–6 people

Ingredients

2 cups whole milk

1 teaspoon vanilla extract

2 cups short-grain rice

⅓ cup whipping cream or *panna di cucina*

2 tablespoons honey

½ teaspoon cinnamon

2 cups mixed berries (blueberries, raspberries, blackberries)

Whipped cream and mint leaves, for garnish

Directions

1. Heat the milk and vanilla extract in a medium saucepan over medium heat and bring to a boil. Add the rice and cook for about 15 minutes, stirring occasionally. Remove from the heat and add the whipping cream, honey, and cinnamon. Refrigerate, covered, for 30 minutes.

2. *Assemble the parfaits in three layers:* Using parfait cups, fill the bottom third of the cups with a layer of the pudding, fill the middle third with a layer of berries, then fill the top third with another layer of pudding. Garnish the top of each cup with a dollop of whipped cream, some more berries, and a mint leaf.

"It is amazing to watch Mom cook and bake so many wonderful things. However, it is rare to see her actually sit down to enjoy the fruits of her labor. But when it comes to rice pudding, her favorite dessert, that's a different matter! Mom often recalls the story of initially discovering rice pudding on her nine-day journey across the Atlantic, when she first came to America. She uses berries because they remind her of the berries blooming along the path to the church. Traditionally, Mom's rice pudding is served in a bowl with a lovely scattering of fruit on top. However, here we have given it a more modern presentation."

— FRANK

NOTE

If you choose to present this dessert in the traditional way, triple the recipe and use a trifle bowl, following the layering steps above. This option is ideal for a party dessert table or a large gathering.

LEMON DOUGHNUTS

(Ciambelline di Lemone)

Ingredients

1 russet potato

½ cup heavy cream

2 teaspoons (1 envelope) active dry yeast

4 cups unbleached all-purpose flour, plus more for dusting

2 jumbo eggs

3 tablespoons sugar

Pinch of salt

4 tablespoons unsalted butter, cubed and softened

Zest of 1 lemon

Juice of 1 lemon or 1 tablespoon lemon extract

3 teaspoons ground cinnamon, for garnish

1 cup vanilla sugar, for garnish

Vegetable oil, for greasing the bowl and for frying

Confectioners' sugar, for garnish

Directions

1. Place the potato in a small saucepan and cover with water. Bring to a boil over medium heat and boil for 8–10 minutes. Drain the potato. When the potato is cool enough to handle, peel, then mash it in a bowl.

2. In a separate saucepan, heat the heavy cream, but do not bring it to a boil. Transfer the cream to a small bowl, add the yeast, and stir until dissolved. Allow the yeast mixture to rest for 20–25 minutes.

3. Pour the flour onto a clean wooden or marble-like surface in a mound and form a well in the center of the flour. In a separate mixing bowl, combine the mashed potato, eggs, sugar, salt, butter, and lemon zest, and whisk together. Pour the egg mixture into the well of the flour, along with the lemon juice, the heavy cream–and–yeast mixture, and ¼ cup of warm water. Using your hands, fold the flour into the mixture until a dough is formed. Place the dough in a lightly oiled bowl, cover, and set aside for 1 hour.

4. Turn over the dough onto a lightly floured surface and knead the dough for 3–4 minutes. Cut one-quarter of the dough and cover the rest of the dough with a kitchen towel.

5. Roll the dough with your hands into a rope about 1 inch wide. Cut the rope into 6-inch pieces and form each piece into a circle, pinching the ends to secure. Place the doughnuts on a baking sheet and cover with a kitchen cloth; set aside in a warm place for 30 minutes to allow the doughnuts to rise. Combine the cinnamon and vanilla sugar in a bowl large enough to hold one doughnut.

6. Pour enough oil into a deep skillet to reach a depth of 3 inches and heat over medium heat until hot. (To see if the oil is ready for frying, add a pinch of dough to the oil; if it bubbles, it is ready.) Place 3–4 doughnuts in the oil (do not overcrowd the pan) and fry, turning once or twice with tongs for even frying, for 30–45 seconds total. Transfer fried doughnuts with tongs to a paper towel–lined wire rack and allow oil to drain briefly. Dip doughnuts while still warm in the sugar mixture and place on a separate wire rack. Garnish with confectioners' sugar and serve warm.

"This is perfect when a friend is coming over for coffee and some *pettegolezzo* (friendly gossip) or as a late-afternoon snack for the children. It is not too sweet and excellent with an espresso, a cup of tea, or a glass of milk."

——ELISA

ALMOND NOUGAT

(Torroncini alle Mandorle)

Ingredients

Unsalted butter, for greasing
the pan

5 cups whole almonds

4 egg whites

2 cups sugar

Juice of 1 lemon

Directions

1. Grease a baking sheet with butter.

2. In a food processor, grind the almonds to the consistency of breadcrumbs and transfer to a bowl. Using an electric stand mixer, fitted with a beater attachment, beat the egg whites and sugar until light and fluffy. Transfer 1 cup of the egg white mixture to a small bowl and set aside.

3. Gradually add the almonds and lemon juice to the egg white in the mixing bowl and beat on medium speed until thoroughly combined. Place the almond mixture on the prepared baking sheet and form with your hands into a rectangular block about 2 inches wide. Use a rolling pin to evenly flatten the top.

4. Preheat the oven to 350°F and line a baking sheet with parchment paper.

5. Using a pastry brush, liberally apply the reserved egg whites to the top of the nougat block. Using a sharp knife, slice the block every ½ inch. Place the slices on the parchment-lined baking sheet and bake for 15–20 minutes. Remove and transfer to a wire rack to cool.

AMARETTO BANANA PIE

(Torta di Amaretti e Banana)

For the pie crust:

2 cups all-purpose flour, plus more for dusting

8 tablespoons salted butter, cubed and softened

3 teaspoons baking powder

2 large eggs

½ cup sugar

1 teaspoon vanilla extract

Solid shortening, for greasing the pie pan

For the amaretto cookies:

3 large eggs, separated

1¼ cups sugar, plus 1 tablespoon

4 cups almond meal flour

1 teaspoon lemon juice

Confectioners' sugar, for coating

For the filling:

3 cups mashed bananas

½ cup brown sugar

2 shots espresso coffee

1 shot dark rum

For the assembly:

12 amaretto cookies, either homemade, per recipe above, or store-bought

2 egg yolks

Directions

1. *Prepare the pie crust:* In a large mixing bowl, combine the flour, butter, and baking powder, and whisk until combined well. In another bowl, beat the eggs, sugar, and vanilla extract. Add the egg mixture to the flour mixture and mix until a silky dough forms. Transfer the dough to a lightly floured surface and knead into a ball. Place the dough in a bowl and refrigerate, covered with plastic wrap, for at least 2 hours.

2. *Prepare the cookies:* Using an electric stand mixer, fitted with a whisk attachment, whisk the egg yolks until fluffy (for approximately 5–7 minutes). Gradually add the sugar, whisking until well blended. Add the almond flour and whisk at low speed (do not overmix)

(for approximately 3–4 minutes). In a separate bowl, beat the egg whites on high speed until soft peaks form (for approximately 5–7 minutes). Using a large rubber spatula, fold one-third of the egg whites into the almond mixture and blend with the spatula. Add the lemon juice and the remaining egg whites and blend until a dough forms. Refrigerate the dough, covered with plastic wrap, for at least 1 hour, or overnight.

3. Preheat the oven to 325°F and line two baking sheets with parchment paper.

4. Place some confectioners' sugar in a small bowl for coating the cookies. Roll the cookie dough into balls the size of small walnuts. Place a few dough balls at a time into the confectioners' sugar and toss to coat well. Arrange 20 balls on each of the lined baking sheets. Bake until lightly golden, about 25–30 minutes. Remove and cool the cookies on a wire rack.

5. Increase the oven temperature to 350°F and grease a deep glass pie pan with solid shortening.

6. Remove your pie dough from the refrigerator and divide it into a 60/40 split. Roll out the smaller portion and line the prepared pie pan with the dough. Evenly distribute the mashed bananas in the pie pan.

7. Place the brown sugar, espresso, and rum in a bowl, and mix thoroughly. Dip each amaretto cookie into the coffee mixture and arrange the cookies in the form of a cross, with space between them. (The cookies go on top of the mashed bananas before you put the top crust of the pie on.) Then add an additional cookie in each section. Pour some of the remaining coffee mixture over the bananas.

8. Roll out the remaining pie dough and cover the pie filling. Seal the edges, cut off any additional dough, and press down with the edge of a fork. Place the egg yolks and a few tablespoons of cold water in a small bowl and beat with a fork to form an egg wash. Brush the top of the pie with some egg wash and bake for 40–45 minutes. Allow to cool before serving.

"You can also subsitute green apples for the bananas, or combine
the two and use store-bought amaretto cookies, if you like."

—ELISA

CREAM PILLOWS

(Pasticciotti)

Makes 2 dozen cookies

Ingredients

For the dough:

4 cups all-purpose flour, plus more for dusting

2 teaspoons baking powder

1 cup of lard or other solid shortening

3 large eggs

1 cup sugar

½ teaspoon vanilla extract

For the cream:

6 egg yolks, reserve the egg whites for brushing the tops

12 tablespoons sugar

6 tablespoons all-purpose flour

3½ cups whole milk

1 (3-inch) cinnamon stick

Whole peel of half a lemon

Unsalted butter, for greasing the pan

Confectioners' sugar, for dusting

Directions

1. In a large mixing bowl, combine flour and baking powder, and whisk well. Add the shortening and cut the shortening into the flour with two knives or a pastry blender until thoroughly blended. In another bowl, whisk together the eggs, sugar, and vanilla extract until combined well. Add the egg mixture to the flour mixture and mix until a silky dough forms. Transfer the dough to a lightly floured surface and knead into a ball. Place the dough in a bowl and refrigerate, covered with plastic wrap, for at least 2 hours.

2. *Prepare the cream:* With an electric stand mixer, fitted with a beater attachment beat the egg yolks and sugar on low speed for 15 minutes. Slowly add the flour and continue to beat on low speed. Pour in the milk and blend thoroughly. Pour the mixture into a medium saucepan and add the cinnamon stick and lemon peel. Bring to a boil over medium heat, stirring continuously. As soon as the first bubbles appear, remove from the heat and transfer to a glass bowl. Remove the cinnamon stick and the lemon peel. Place wax paper directly on the surface of the filling, to prevent a film from forming, and refrigerate until you are ready to use, at least 1 hour.

3. Preheat the oven to 350°F and grease the cups of a mini muffin tin or individual tartlet cups with shortening or oil.

4. Remove the dough from the refrigerator. Divide the dough into two equal-sized pieces. Roll out one piece of dough on a lightly floured surface to a ⅛-inch thickness. Use a small drinking glass to cut out rounds large enough to line the mini muffin tin cups or tartlet cups. Place the pastry dough rounds into the pans and press down and along the edges. Fill each shell three-fourths full with the cream.

5. Roll out the remaining piece of dough to a ⅛-inch thickness and cut into rounds large enough to cover the tops of the cups in the pan or the tartlet cups. Seal shut by pressing on the edges, bringing the bottom pastry dough together with the top.

6. Brush the tops of the pastry dough with some egg white and bake for 20–25 minutes, or until lightly golden. Remove from the oven and allow the pastries to cool before removing from the pan or tartlet cups. Carefully turn over the pan or tartlet cups and gently remove the pastries. Allow to cool completely on a wire rack. Garnish tops with some sifted confectioners' sugar.

Chapter Seven

SAUCES, CONDIMENTS, AND PRESERVES

(SALSE, CONDIMENTI E CONSERVE)

SISTERS STIRRING THE POT

lost my only sister, Dorina, when she passed away while giving birth. I was just fourteen years old at the time, and the experience of her death is something that I have carried with me ever since. Over the course of my life, though, I have also had the great fortune to form close bonds with nine women who became my sisters-in-law. I still think of Dorina often and miss her very much, even today. Yet, the love and affection these women and I have shared has helped to heal the pain of losing my own sister.

Two of my childhood friends, Iola and Pierina, became my sisters-in-law when they each married one of my brothers. Iola always had big dreams of the city, and she found an opportunity for herself and my brother Vincenzo to start a new life in Rome. On the other hand, Pierina, who married my brother Joe, was like me: She had no desire to leave our little town and was more than content with the simple life. Pierina's mother died during her birth, so she was raised by her father. But during those moments in life when a young lady needs her mother, my own mother assumed that role. (Years later when I was not able to reach my own mother in time, Pierina was by her side as she took her last breath.) When I went to cook with my Zia Ida at a young age, Pierina apprenticed with the local seamstress and learned to sew. Pierina and I were born only a month apart, and a day did not go by that we were not together. Then, ironically, she and my brother Joe decided to be the first of our family to move to America. Suddenly, for the first time in twenty years, Pierina was thousands of miles away.

After Vincenzo moved away with Iola, and Joe and Pierina emigrated to America, I was left alone to ponder the future. Luckily, I would soon marry Francesco and move to his village to live with his parents and four sisters. When I arrived, the two eldest, Iole and Giuseppina, both extremely talented seamstresses, were in charge of the household and worked very hard to help support their family. They left the house early each morning to go work at the factory, while my mother-in-law joined the other women in the village to work in the fields. I stayed home with the responsibility of caring for Francesco's two younger sisters, Concetta and Adina. Caring for them was really my first experience with motherhood.

I have heard people say that relationships with in-laws often can be strained and difficult. Indeed, jealousy could have easily ruined my relationship with Francesco's four sisters. After all, I had won the affection of the only male child in the household. His sisters adored their older brother, and to them he was free of defects, perfect in every way. Even today, to hear Giuseppina describe him as tall and dark, with a full head of hair—when, in fact, Francesco was quite short and began balding at a young age—proves that true love is blind. Although there were certainly some hard times, especially when I first arrived, I would have to say that I was extremely blessed to count these four women and my new mother as family. We quickly formed sisterly bonds that erased whatever differences we had at the beginning of our journey together.

When Francesco and I made the decision to move to America, his mother was pregnant with another child, and his father had just passed away due to an accident. It was difficult to leave my mother-in-law with four girls to raise and one on the way. Many people in our village, not knowing why we would cast such a fate on this poor woman and our family, did not support us and literally turned their backs on us as we left town. But Francesco persisted, convinced that he could find better jobs and wages in America. With the gift of hindsight, I can say that Francesco was absolutely right. At the time, however, this was a bold decision, and while I was very proud of his determination, I did not agree with the idea of moving to America.

Francesco's youngest sister, Franca, was born after we arrived in America. I was somewhat heartened by reuniting with Pierina, but at the same time, I was now thousands of miles away from the four women who had become my family. We wanted very badly for them all to move to America, but this would never happen. The process of bringing them to America was long, and eventually they all married and found lives of their own in Italy, forcing us to maintain a long-distance relationship for many years. Francesco continually made sure that his mother and sisters were cared for, even if we had to sacrifice. He was unable to attend their weddings, but sent back funds to purchase their wedding dresses.

As fate would have it, my two younger brothers, Nicola and Nino, eventually married and moved with their brides to America. When they first arrived, I could see the terror in my new sisters-in-law, Maria and Elvira; it was the same mix of fear and doubt I felt myself when I first came to America. My parents had already come to America, and these young girls were meeting them for the first time. And so, Pierina and I took it upon ourselves to make sure our new family members were welcomed with open arms and had happy lives in America. Preparing

weekly Sunday dinners together played an important role in our bonding. Some say that too many chefs in the kitchen spoil the stew. I would say it was quite the opposite. We all lived a happy and full life in America, doing the best we could to raise our families in this strange land. These women were an important safety net that helped me survive hard times, and I can only hope that I was able to return their kindness, even a little bit.

Eventually, my parents, Joe and Nino, and their families, all returned to Italy, leaving Maria and me behind. To this day, we continue the tradition of Sunday dinner, and we celebrate holiday dinners at our respective homes on a rotating basis—a tradition we are only now slowly handing over to our children. Maria and I also went on to work together for many years, doing what we do best—cooking. As sisters, we were alone, but it only strengthened our bond. We stuck together and defended each other whenever the need arose.

Living so far away from my other sisters was a true test of our family bonds, although, truly, these bonds never felt strained. The sisterhood I formed with these women would prove more powerful than the distance between us. Francesco's youngest sister, Franca, was just a year younger than my own daughter, Nadia, and so it was actually quite natural to bond with her. Francesco and I treated her like a daughter, making sure she was given all the opportunities available to her. Franca has since become a very talented ceramics painter in Italy. She also willingly took on the responsibility of caring for her mother until her death, a duty that should have rightfully fallen to me. I am unbelievably grateful for her sacrifice, which has strengthened our already strong connection.

Over the years, I have lost Adina, Iola, and Pierina, who died in 2013, like Francesco. That year began with the loss of Pierina, then my dear friend Elena, my mother-in-law, Joe, and, finally, Francesco at Christmas. Throughout these difficult times, Maria never left my side, and for months after Francesco's death, she spent the long nights with me, many times with her arms around me as I cried myself to sleep. And although I may live an ocean apart from Iole, Giuseppina, Concetta, Elvira, and Franca, my bonds with these ladies is as strong as it is with Maria, who lives less than five minutes away. We look forward to the times we are able to spend together now. Recently, Elvira and Giuseppina accompanied me on a tour of Tuscany to promote my first cookbook. It had been a few months since we had seen each other in person, but we had talked on the phone many times in between, and the marvels of the Internet provided opportunities to video-chat with one another. Once back in each other's company, we were able to pick up exactly where we had left off. This is not at all hard to do with people one considers family. These women are not my sisters-in-law. They are my sisters and my best friends. *Amore per la famiglia!*

BLACK TRUFFLE AND MUSHROOM CREAM SAUCE

(Sugo di Tartufo Nero e Crema di Funghi)

This sauce accompanies about 1 pound of pasta

½ cup salted butter

½ pound Porcini mushrooms, chopped

1 cup frozen green peas

3 garlic cloves, chopped

Pinch of salt and black pepper

1 cup dry white wine

¼ cup chopped fresh parsley

4 cups heavy cream

2 tablespoons grated fresh black truffles

½ cup freshly grated Parmesan and Pecorino Romano cheese, for garnish

Melt the butter in a large sauté pan over medium-high heat, then add the mushrooms, peas, garlic, and a pinch of salt and pepper, and sauté for 8–10 minutes. Add the wine and parsley and sauté for 5 minutes more. Reduce the heat, then add the heavy cream and 1 tablespoon grated truffles, and simmer for 10 minutes, until the sauce thickens. Remove from the heat and let the mixture stand for 5 minutes. When plated, garnish with cheese and the remaining tablespoon of grated truffles.

ASPARAGUS AND PANCETTA SAUCE

(Sugo di Asparagi e Pancetta)

This sauce accompanies about 1 pound of pasta

½ pound pancetta, chopped

½ cup olive oil

½ large Spanish onion, chopped

6 cups halved cherry tomatoes

1 small bunch asparagus, cut into 1-inch pieces

1. In a large sauté pan, sauté pancetta over medium heat for 10 minutes. Drain grease from the pan and add the olive oil. Add the onion and sauté for 5 minutes, then add the tomatoes and simmer for 20–25 minutes.

2. Fill a saucepan with water and bring to a boil, then add asparagus and boil for 5–7 minutes. Drain asparagus, reserving 1 cup of asparagus water, then add asparagus and the cup of asparagus water to the onion and tomato mixture. Sauté for 5 minutes more. Serve over your favorite pasta.

CREAMY ALFREDO BASIL SAUCE

(Sugo con Panna e Basilico)

This sauce accompanies about 1 pound of pasta

8 tablespoons salted butter

2 tablespoons olive oil

2 garlic cloves, minced

4 cups heavy cream

2 cups finely chopped fresh basil

1 teaspoon black pepper

1 tablespoon all-purpose flour

GRATED TRUFFLES

HOT RED PEPPERS

JALAPENOS

HOT GARDEN PEPPERS

ABRUZZESE VEGETABLE SPREAD

ROASTED PEPPERS

2 cups freshly grated Parmesan cheese

1 cup freshly grated Pecorino Romano cheese

In a medium saucepan, melt the butter with the olive oil over medium-low heat. Add the garlic, cream, basil, and pepper, and bring the mixture to a simmer. Add the flour and the cheeses, and simmer for 8–10 minutes more, or until the sauce has thickened and is smooth. Remove from the heat and let it stand for 5 minutes before adding to pasta.

BOLOGNESE SAUCE

(Ragu alla Bolognese)

This sauce accompanies about 1 pound of pasta

¼ cup olive oil

3 garlic cloves

1 medium onion, chopped

1 pound lean ground beef

1 cup red wine

1 carrot, peeled and finely chopped

1 stalk celery, finely chopped

½ cup panna di cucina or heavy cream

2 (28-ounce) cans tomato purée

1 teaspoon salt, plus more to taste

2–3 fresh basil leaves

Pinch of black pepper

In a large sauté pan with a lid, heat the olive oil and garlic over medium heat, then add the onion and sauté for 5–7 minutes. Add the ground beef and cook until brown. Drain grease from the pan. Add the wine, carrot, celery, *panna* or heavy cream, tomato purée, salt, basil, and pepper, and simmer over low heat, partially covered, for 1 hour. Stir occasionally. Add salt to taste. Serve over your favorite pasta.

PESTO

(Pesto alla Genovese)

This sauce accompanies about 1 pound of pasta

2 cups chopped fresh basil leaves, without stems

3 garlic cloves

¾ cup olive oil

Pinch of salt

½ cup freshly grated Parmesan cheese

¼ cup freshly grated Pecorino Romano cheese

Place the basil and garlic in a food processor and blend until minced, then continue to blend as you slowly add the oil. Add a pinch of salt and the cheeses, and blend thoroughly. Transfer pesto to a bowl, cover the surface directly with plastic wrap, and refrigerate. Remove pesto from refrigerator 30 minutes before using to return to room temperature. Serve over your favorite pasta or on toasted bread.

AMATRICANA SAUCE

(Sugo all' Amatriciana)

This sauce accompanies about 1 pound of pasta

¼ cup olive oil

3 garlic cloves, whole

1 pound bacon, chopped

2 Spanish onions, chopped

2 (28-ounce) cans crushed tomatoes with basil

½ cup chopped fresh parsley

½ cup chopped fresh basil

Pinch of salt

Freshly grated Pecorino Romano cheese, for garnish

In a saucepan, heat the olive oil and garlic over medium heat, then add the bacon and onions, and sauté for 10 minutes. Reduce heat, then add the crushed tomatoes, parsley, basil, and a pinch of salt, and simmer for 1 hour, stirring occasionally. Keep a cup of water nearby and occasionally add some water to keep the sauce from thickening too much. Serve over your favorite pasta and garnish with cheese.

MUSHROOM AND PANCETTA SAUCE

(Sugo di Funghi e Pancetta)

This sauce accompanies about 1 pound of pasta

¼ cup olive oil

2 cups cubed pancetta

16 tablespoons unsalted butter

¼ cup dry white wine

4 cups finely chopped mixed mushrooms

Pinch of salt

Freshly grated Pecorino Romano cheese, for garnish

In a sauté pan, heat the oil and pancetta over medium heat, and sauté pancetta for 5–7 minutes. Add the butter, wine, mushrooms, and a pinch of salt, and continue to sauté for 10 minutes more until mushrooms are tender. Pour over your favorite pasta and garnish with cheese.

"This is a simple twenty-minute sauce, perfect for any kind of pasta dish. It is usually served in the summer months al fresco."

—ELISA

TOMATO RICOTTA SAUCE

(Sugo di Pomodoro e Ricotta)

This sauce accompanies about 1 pound of pasta

¼ cup olive oil

2–3 garlic cloves

2 (28-ounce) cans, crushed tomatoes

1 teaspoon chopped fresh parsley

1 teaspoon chopped fresh basil

Salt, to taste

16 ounces Ricotta cheese, drained

¼ cup freshly grated Pecorino Romano cheese

In a saucepan, heat the olive oil and garlic over medium heat. Reduce the heat, then add the tomatoes, parsley, basil, and salt, and simmer for 1 hour, stirring occasionally. Add the Ricotta cheese and continue to simmer for 15–20 minutes more. Serve over your favorite pasta and garnish with Pecorino Romano cheese.

TOMATO CREAM SAUCE

(Sugo di Pomodoro e Panna)

This sauce accompanies about 1 pound of pasta

¼ cup olive oil

2 garlic cloves, minced

2 (28-ounce) cans crushed tomatoes

Pinch of dried basil, oregano, and parsley

2 teaspoons crushed hot red pepper flakes, or jarred red peppers, plus more for garnish

1 pint heavy cream

1 cup freshly grated Parmesan cheese, plus more for garnish

½ cup freshly grated Pecorino Romano cheese, plus more for garnish

1. In a large sauté pan, heat the olive oil and garlic over medium heat for 2–3 minutes. Add the crushed tomatoes, basil, oregano, parsley, and red pepper flakes, and bring to a boil.

2. As the tomatoes begin to boil, reduce the heat, add the heavy cream and cheeses, and simmer, stirring to mix thoroughly for a few minutes. Remove from the heat. Serve immediately over your favorite pasta and garnish with more cheese and red pepper flakes to taste.

TUNA AND ANCHOVY SAUCE

(Sugo di Tonno e Acciughe)

This sauce accompanies about 1 pound of pasta

4 pounds fresh tomatoes, or 2 (28-ounce) cans crushed tomatoes

¾ cup olive oil

1 whole small onion (see Note below)

2 garlic cloves, chopped

2 celery stalks, finely chopped

¼ cup chopped fresh parsley, including the stems

3–4 bay leaves

Salt and fresh black pepper, to taste

½ cup chopped black olives

½ cup chopped green olives

8–10 anchovies, chopped

2 5-ounce cans tuna fish in olive oil, drained

1. If using fresh tomatoes, boil water in a saucepan and add the tomatoes. When the skin begins to wrinkle, remove the tomatoes. Let them cool. Peel the skin and chop them into small pieces.

2. In a large stockpot, place the oil, the whole onion, and the garlic, and sauté until the onion and garlic are light golden in color. Add the tomatoes, celery, parsley, bay leaves, and salt and pepper to taste, and bring to a boil, uncovered, over medium heat.

3. When the water boils, reduce heat, then add 1 cup of water and simmer for 1 hour, until the sauce thickens. Add the olives, anchovies, and tuna, and continue to simmer for 10 minutes more, stirring occasionally. Serve over your favorite pasta.

NOTE: The whole onion will break up in the sauce and flavor it. When we serve this sauce over pasta we do not include any large chunks of the onion.

CHERRY TOMATO AND MUSHROOM SAUCE

(Sugo di Pomodorini e Funghi)

This sauce accompanies about 1 pound of pasta

2 tablespoons olive oil, plus ¼ cup more to finish the sauce

2 garlic cloves, minced

4 cups chopped mushrooms

6 cups halved cherry tomatoes

½ cup chopped fresh parsley

1 teaspoon salt

In a large sauté pan, heat 2 tablespoons of olive oil and the garlic over medium heat, then add the mushrooms and sauté for 15–20 minutes. Add the tomatoes, parsley, and salt, and continue to sauté for 10 minutes more, stirring occasionally. Pour over pasta, then pour one ladleful of pasta water and ¼ cup of olive oil over the sauce and toss thoroughly.

"The cherry tomato and mushroom sauce is a simple summer sauce shared with me by my sister-in-law, Elvira. It is very refreshing and served best with short pasta."

—ELISA

"The red pepper cream spread is a simple dipping sauce I created for some of Mom's amazing antipasti. I also use this sauce to top my crab cakes."

—FRANK

ROASTED RED PEPPER CREAM SPREAD

(Crema di Peperoni Arrostiti)

Serves 4–6 people

2 large red roasting peppers

2 tablespoons olive oil

½ cup chopped fresh parsley

2–3 garlic cloves, chopped

½ teaspoon salt

1 ½ cups mayonnaise

1. Preheat the oven to 400°F.

2. Cut the peppers into quarters and remove the stems and seeds. Place peppers, skin side up, on a baking sheet and bake for 1 hour, until the skin is wrinkled. Remove peppers from the oven and cool until easy to handle. Peel away the skin and cut the flesh into ¼-inch strips. Allow the peppers to cool completely.

3. Place peppers in a food processor, add the olive oil, parsley, garlic, and salt, and blend until creamy. Transfer mixture to a bowl. Add the mayonnaise and fold into the pepper mixture. Refrigerate, covered with plastic wrap, for 30 minutes before using as a dipping sauce.

PICKLED ONIONS

(Cipolline)

Fills 4–5 (1/2-pint) mason jars

4 cups cipollini or pearl onions

6 chili or long red hot peppers, seeded and cut into ¼-inch-thick slices

2 cups olive oil

2 garlic cloves, minced

4 teaspoons sugar

2 teaspoons black pepper

3 cups red wine vinegar

12 fresh basil leaves, chopped

1 bay leaf, chopped

Shaved Parmesan cheese, freshly grated, for garnish

1. Peel the outer layers of the onions and remove the base of the cipollini onions. Place the onions in a large glass bowl. Add the sliced peppers, olive oil, garlic, sugar, and black pepper, and cover with water. Let mixture soak for 4–6 hours.

2. In a medium saucepan, place the vinegar, basil, and bay leaf, and bring to a slow boil over medium heat. Remove from the heat and allow to cool. Drain the onions and peppers well and set aside.

3. *Sterilize your jars and lids:* Wash the jars, lids, and screw bands in hot, soapy water. Rinse well and dry the screw bands. Place the jars on a wire rack in a

large pot with a lid and add enough water to cover them by 2 inches. Cover the pot, bring the water to a boil, and boil the jars for 10 minutes. Remove from the heat and keep the jars submerged in the water. Place the jar lids in a small saucepan with a lid and cover the jar lids with water. Heat the water to 180°F (do not boil), then remove from heat and cover the pan. Keep the lids submerged in water until ready to use. When ready to use, carefully remove jars and lids from water and allow them to completely cool. Reserve water in pot.

4. Spoon the onions and peppers into the jars, filling to the base of the neck of the jars. Pour the vinegar mixture over the onions, pressing down to release any air bubbles and tightly seal the lids.

5. Return the jars to the pot of water and boil until your lids have sealed tightly, 20–30 minutes, depending on the size of your jars. Carefully remove the jars from the water, giving the lids a tight twist, and let cool. Store preserves in a dry place. Once opened, refrigerate the jar until the onions are fully consumed.

GIARDINIERA

Fills 2 (16-ounce) mason jars

2 red bell peppers, cut into ¼-inch-thick slices

2 celery stalks, cut into ½-inch slices

4 chili peppers, seeded and cut into ½-inch slices

1 cup sliced or shredded carrots

1 cauliflower, cut into florets

½ cup pitted green olives

½ cup salt

3 cloves garlic, minced

1 tablespoon black pepper

1 cup distilled white vinegar, plus more for topping off the jars

1 cup olive oil

1. Combine the peppers, celery, chilies, carrots, cauliflower, and olives in a large mixing bowl. Add the salt and stir into the vegetables. Cover the vegetables with water and refrigerate, covered with plastic wrap, for 24 hours.

2. Drain and rinse the vegetables under cold running water to remove the salt. Mix the garlic, black pepper, vinegar, and olive oil in a large bowl, add the vegetables, and blend thoroughly. Refrigerate the vegetable mixture, covered with plastic wrap, for 2–3 days.

3. When the vegetables have marinated for 2–3 days, sterilize your jars and lids (see page 227).

4. Remove the vegetables from the refrigerator and bring to room temperature. Ladle the vegetables into the jars, pressing down firmly to remove any air bubbles, and tightly seal the lids. Top the jars with more white vinegar. Press down to release any air bubbles and tightly seal the lids.

5. Return the jars to the pot of water and boil until your lids have sealed tightly, 20–30 minutes, depending on the size of your jars. Carefully remove jars from the water, giving the lids a tight twist, and let cool. Store preserves in a dry place. Once opened, refrigerate the jar until the vegetables are fully consumed.

"Giardiniera is a mix of pickled cauliflower, carrots, and peppers. Giardiniera is also called *sott'aceto*, which means 'under vinegar,' a common term for pickled foods. This is a wonderful antipasta, or it can be served as a side dish for a summer evening dinner."

—ELISA

PICKLED EGGPLANT IN VINEGAR

(Melanzane Sott'Aceto)

Fills 3–4 (16-ounce) mason jars

8 cups white wine vinegar

1 cup water

¼ cup sugar

¼ cup of salt

8–10 eggplants

3 cups olive oil, plus more for topping the jars

1 cup fresh oregano, chopped

½ cup red pepper flakes

Pinch of salt

1. In a large bowl, mix together the vinegar, water, sugar, and salt. Remove skin from the eggplants and cut the eggplants into ¼-inch slices. Place eggplant slices in the vinegar mixture and cover bowl with plastic wrap. Set aside for 24 hours.

2. Drain the eggplant. Arrange slices on a clean kitchen towel, then roll up the towel, pressing firmly as you roll to drain the eggplant of any remaining vinegar. Place the eggplant in a bowl. Add the 3 cups of olive oil, oregano, red pepper flakes, and a pinch of salt, and mix thoroughly.

3. *Sterilize your jars and lids* (see page 227).

4. Ladle the eggplant into the jars, pressing down firmly to remove any air bubbles. Top with olive oil and tightly seal the lids. Return the jars to the pot of water and boil until your lids have sealed tightly, 20–30 minutes, depending on the size of your jars. Carefully remove the jars from the water, giving the lids a tight twist, and let cool. Store preserves in a dry place. Once opened, refrigerate the jar until the eggplant is fully consumed.

PICKLED ZUCCHINI

(Zucchine Sott'Aceto)

Fills about 2 (16-ounce) jars

4 pounds small green zucchini

¼ cup olive oil, plus more for topping the jars

3 garlic cloves, minced

¼ cup finely chopped fresh parsley

2 tablespoons white vinegar

1 tablespoon salt

1. Julienne the zucchini lengthwise using a mandoline and place the zucchini in a medium-sized saucepan. Add the ¼ cup olive oil, garlic, parsley, vinegar, and salt, and mix to combine. Add 5 cups of water, bring to a boil, and boil zucchini for 5–7 minutes. Drain and allow to cool completely. Set mixture aside.

2. *Sterilize your jars and lids* (see page 227).

3. Spoon the zucchini into the jars, pressing down firmly to remove any air bubbles. Top up the jars with olive oil and tightly seal the lids.

4. Return the jars to the pot of water and boil

until your lids have sealed tightly, 20–30 minutes, depending on the size of your jars. Carefully remove the jars from the water, giving the lids a tight twist, and let cool. Store preserves in a dry place. Once opened, refrigerate the jar until the zucchini is fully consumed.

SALTED GREEN TOMATOES

(Pomodori Verdi Salati)

Fills 4–5 (½-pint) mason jars or 3 (1-pint) mason jars

5 pounds green tomatoes

2–4 cups coarse sea salt

20 garlic cloves, chopped

½ cup fennel seed

Olive oil

1. If you are using the larger jars, clean the tomatoes and cut them into ½-inch slices; if you are using the smaller jars, clean the tomatoes, cut them into ½-inch slices, and then cut them in half again.

2. Using a clean ceramic planter pot with drainage, place the tomatoes in the planter a few at a time, adding some of the sea salt, garlic, and fennel seed as you go, until the tomatoes are evenly coated.

3. Place plastic wrap directly on top of the tomatoes and press down firmly to press the tomatoes down into the pot. Using a plate about the same size as the pot, place it over the plastic wrap and continue to press down on the tomatoes. Place something heavy, but not metallic, on the plate to keep the tomatoes sealed.

4. Place the pot outdoors, out of direct sunlight and on an elevated surface, appropriate for the tomatoes to drain, for two weeks. All the water from the tomatoes will drain from the holes in your pot.

5. After two weeks, remove the tomatoes from the pot, brush off any remaining garlic and fennel seed, and transfer the tomatoes to a bowl.

6. *Sterilize your jars and lids* (see page 227).

7. Place the tomatoes in layers in the jars, pressing down firmly to remove any air bubbles and adding some salt, fennel, and garlic to each layer. Give the tomatoes a final press and top up the jars with olive oil. Tightly seal the lids.

8. Return jars to the pot of water and boil until your lids have sealed tightly, 20–30 minutes, depending on the size of your jars. Carefully remove jars from the water, giving the lids a tight twist, and let them cool. Store preserves in a dry place. Once opened, refrigerate the jar until the tomatoes are fully consumed.

"Preparing these green tomatoes is a tradition that reinforces the idea that nothing should go to waste. Many times we would have late-blooming tomatoes in the garden, but it was so late in the season that they would not have time to ripen. So we would pick them hard and green, and preserve them for the winter months. Every September or so, I still use up my green tomatoes by preparing this simple preserve."

—*Elisa*

HOT PEPPER SPREAD

(Patè di Peperoncini)

Yield varies with size of peppers; use 4-ounce
jars or small mason jars

2–3 dozen red hot long peppers (see Note below)

½ cup olive oil

Pinch of salt

1. Cut the peppers in half and remove the seeds and
the inner lining. Place the peppers in a blender with
½ cup of the oil and a pinch of salt, and blend (do
not liquefy).

2. *If using 4-ounce baby food jars:* Wash the jars and
lids in hot, soapy water. Rinse well and dry. Place the
jars and lids in a large saucepan with a lid and add
enough water to cover them by 2 inches. Cover the
pan, bring the water to a boil, and boil jars and lids
for 10 minutes. Remove jars and lids and allow them
to completely cool.

3. *If using mason jars, sterilize your jars and lids*
according to instructions on page 227.

4. Spoon the pepper purée into the jars, pressing
down firmly to remove any air bubbles. Top up the
jars with some olive oil and tightly seal the lids.

5. Return the jars to the pot of water and boil
until your lids have sealed tightly, 20–30 minutes,
depending on the size of your jars. Carefully remove
jars from the water, giving the lids a tight twist, and
let cool. Store preserves in a dry place. Once opened,
refrigerate the jar until the pepper spread is fully
consumed.

   Note: We buy "red hots" pepper plants and use
these long, skinny peppers for this spread, but you
can use chili peppers or any other hot red peppers.

JARRED TOMATOES

(Pomodori Pelati)

Fills 4 (16-ounce) mason jars

4 pounds fresh tomatoes

½ cup olive oil

4 garlic cloves, halved

2 cups chopped fresh basil

½ cup salt

1. Boil water in a stockpot and add tomatoes. When
the skin begins to wrinkle, remove tomatoes. Allow
the tomatoes to cool, then peel and chop them into
small pieces.

2. In a large stockpot, heat the oil and garlic and sauté
for 4–5 minutes. Add the tomatoes, basil, and salt,
and simmer for 1 hour.

3. *Sterilize your jars and lids* (see page 227).

4. Ladle the tomatoes into sterilized jars, pressing down firmly to remove any air bubbles and tightly seal the lids. Return the jars to the pot of water and boil until your lids have sealed tightly, 20–30 minutes, depending on the size of your jars. Carefully remove the jars from the water, giving the lids a tight twist, and let cool. Store preserves in a dry place. Once opened, refrigerate the jar until tomatoes are fully consumed.

ROASTED RED PEPPERS

(Peperoni Arrosto)

Fills 3–4 (8-ounce) mason jars

4 large red roasting peppers

½ cup olive oil

¼ cup fresh parsley, chopped

2–3 garlic cloves, chopped

½ teaspoon salt

1. Preheat the oven to 400°F.

2. Cut the peppers into quarters and remove the stem and seeds. Place peppers, skin side up, on a baking sheet and bake for 1 hour, until skin is wrinkled. Remove peppers from the oven and cool to room temperature. Peel away skin and cut peppers into ¼-inch strips. Place peppers in a bowl, add the olive oil, parsley, garlic, and salt, and mix well. Marinate the peppers, covered with plastic wrap, for 1 hour before jarring.

3. *Sterilize your jars and lids* (see page 227).

4. Ladle peppers into the jars and top up with some olive oil from the marinade, pressing down firmly to remove any air bubbles and tightly seal the lids. Return the jars to the pot of water and boil until your lids have sealed tightly, 20–30 minutes, depending on the size of your jars. Carefully remove the jars from the water, giving the lids a tight twist, and let cool. Store preserves in a dry place. Once opened, refrigerate the jar until peppers are fully consumed.

ABRUZZESE VEGETABLE SPREAD

(Conserva Abruzzesi)

Fills 3 (8-ounce) mason jars

"This is an excellent condiment to flavor sauces and meats, or to simply use on its own on some fresh toasted bread. We would prepare this during the summer for the winter months when fresh vegetables were scarce."

—*Elisa*

4 carrots, chopped

3 celery stalks, chopped

1 Spanish onion, chopped

4 garlic cloves, chopped

½ cup chopped fresh parsley, including the stems

2 tablespoons salt

1 cup olive oil, plus more for topping up the jars

1. Place the carrots, celery, onion, garlic, parsley, and salt in a food processor, and blend to a thick paste. Slowly add 1 cup of the olive oil and continue to blend until thoroughly mixed.

2. *Sterilize your jars and lids* (see page 227).

3. Spoon the mixture into your jars, pressing down firmly to remove any air bubbles. Top up the jars with olive oil and tightly seal the lids. Return the jars to the pot of water and boil until your lids have sealed tightly, 20–30 minutes, depending on the size of your jars. Carefully remove the jars from the water, giving the lids a tight twist, and let cool. Store preserves in a dry place. Once opened, refrigerate the jar until the spread is fully consumed.

APRICOT JAM

(Marmellata di Albicocche)

Fills 2–3 (½-pint) mason jars

1 dozen ripe apricots

1 cup sugar

¼ cup lemon juice

1 tablespoon lemon zest

1 teaspoon vanilla extract

1 tablespoon dark rum

1. Cut the apricots in half and remove the pits, then cut the apricots into bite-size pieces and place in a saucepan. Add the sugar, lemon juice, zest, and vanilla extract, and blend thoroughly.

2. Bring apricots to a boil over medium heat, stirring frequently to keep the mixture from burning and sticking to the pot. Add the rum, reduce the heat,

and continue to simmer for 15–20 minutes, stirring occasionally. Remove from the heat and set aside.

3. *Sterilize your jars and lids* (see page 227).

4. Spoon the jam into your jars, pressing down firmly to remove any air bubbles and tightly seal the lids. Return the jars to the pot of water and boil until your lids have sealed tightly, 20–30 minutes, depending on the size of your jars. Carefully remove the jars from the water, giving the lids a tight twist, and let cool. Store your jam in a dry place for up to 1 year. Once opened, you must refrigerate the jar until jam is fully consumed.

STRAWBERRY JAM

(Marmellata di Fragole)

Fills 2 (½-pint) mason jars

Ingredients

2 pounds fresh strawberries, hulled and cut into quarters

2 cups sugar

½ cup lemon juice

1 tablespoon vanilla extract

1 tablespoon lemon zest

1 tablespoon orange zest

1. Place the strawberries in a saucepan and add the sugar, lemon juice, vanilla extract, and zests, and blend thoroughly. Bring to a boil over medium heat, stirring frequently to keep the mixture from burning and sticking to the pot. Reduce the heat, then mash the strawberries with a masher and simmer for 20–25 minutes, stirring occasionally. Remove from the heat and set aside.

2. Sterilize your jars and lids (see page 227).

3. Spoon the strawberries into your jars, pressing down firmly to remove any air bubbles and tightly seal the lids. Return the jars to the pot of water and boil until your lids have sealed tightly, 20–30 minutes, depending on the size of your jars. Carefully remove the jars from the water, giving the lids a tight twist, and let cool. Store your jam in a dry place for up to 1 year. Once opened, you must refrigerate the jar until the jam is fully consumed.

FIG JAM
(Marmellata di Fichi)

Fills 2 (1-pint) mason jars

4 cups peeled and chopped fresh figs

3 cups sugar

$1/2$ cup grape juice

$1/2$ cup lemon juice

1 tablespoon lemon zest

2 cinnamon sticks

1. Combine the figs, sugar, grape and lemon juices, lemon zest, and cinnamon sticks in a large saucepan, and bring to a boil over medium heat, stirring frequently to keep the mixture from burning and sticking to the pot. Reduce the heat, then mash the figs with a masher, and simmer the mixture, stirring occasionally, for 20–25 minutes, until the jam thickens. Remove from the heat and set aside.

2. *Sterilize your jars and lids* (see page 227).

3. Remove the cinnamon sticks and lemon zest from the fig mixture and spoon the figs into your jars, pressing down firmly to remove any air bubbles and

tightly seal the lids. Return the jars to the pot of water and boil until your lids have sealed tightly, 20–30 minutes, depending on the size of your jars. Carefully remove the jars from the water, giving the lids a tight twist, and let cool. Store your jam in a dry place for up to 1 year. Once opened, you must refrigerate the jar until the jam is fully consumed.

"Francesco's home in San Massimo was surrounded by fig and nut trees. Figs were always my favorite summer treat, and I always seemed to eat too many and regretted it later. These fig trees provided shade when we dined al fresco in the summertime, and they have provided our family with this jam for decades. Recently, after Francesco's death, we came across his treasure of photographs. Included in this collection were some photographs that he had taken of our grandchildren climbing these very same trees, as well as a photo of Francesco under these trees just months before his death. When I was a young girl and first met Francesco, he had a love of photography and his own camera. Owning a camera was still very rare in those days. On our wedding day, I dreamed of having many, many photos, only to find out that he had sold his camera to buy me a wedding gift. He continued his passion for taking photos throughout his life."

—ELISA

PRESERVED PEARS

(Pere Conservate)

Fills 3 (16-ounce) mason jars

2–3 pounds ripe Bartlett pears

1/2 cup fresh lemon juice

2 cups sugar

1 teaspoon vanilla extract

1 stick cinnamon

1. Peel the pears and remove the cores. Quarter the pears, place them in a large bowl of water with the lemon juice, and allow them to soak for 2 hours.

2. Drain the pears. In a saucepan, place 8 cups of water, the sugar, vanilla extract, and cinnamon, and bring to a boil. Add the pears and boil for 5–10 minutes. Remove from the heat and set aside. Discard the cinnamon stick.

3. *Sterilize your jars and lids* (see page 227).

4. Spoon the pears into your jars to fill them three-fourths full, pressing down firmly to remove any air bubbles. Fill the top quarter of the jar with the juice from the pot and tightly seal the lids.

5. Return the jars to the pot of water and boil until your lids have sealed tightly, 20–30 minutes, depending on the size of your jars. Carefully remove the jars from the water, giving the lids a tight twist, and let cool. Store your pears in a dry place for up to 1 year. Once opened, you must refrigerate the jar until the pears are fully consumed.

PRESERVED PEACHES

(Pesche Conservate)

Fills 3 (16-ounce) mason jars

2–3 pounds peaches

2 tablespoons of honey

3 cups sugar

1. Bring a large saucepan of water to a boil. Wash and drain the peaches, then drop the peaches into the boiling water for 1 minute. Remove the peaches with a strainer and rinse them under cold running water. Peel off the skins, and cut the peaches into quarters, discarding the pits. Retain the water in the saucepan.

2. Place the honey and 4 cups of the boiling water in a bowl. Drop a few peach quarters at a time into the bowl and allow them to soak for 2–3 minutes. Remove with a slotted spoon and drain on a wire rack.

3. *Prepare the syrup:* In a saucepan, heat 4 cups of water and the sugar over medium heat, stirring until the sugar is dissolved. Remove from the heat.

4. *Sterilize your jars and lids* (see page 227).

5. Spoon the peaches into your jars to fill them three-quarters full, pressing down firmly to remove any air bubbles. Fill the top of the jar with syrup, pressing down to release air, and tightly seal the lids.

6. Return the jars to the pot of water and boil until your lids have sealed properly, 20–30 minutes, depending on the size of your jars. Carefully remove the jars from the water, giving the lids a tight twist, and let cool. Store your peaches in a dry place for up to 1 year. Once opened, you must refrigerate the jar until the preserves are fully consumed.

In the End

I sometimes feel guilty that I have found this new purpose and fortune so late in life. I still ask myself, Why me? And I wonder, What would my Francesco say? Then, one day, a dear friend of his told me that Francesco would be happy that I am smiling again, and that it was my smile that attracted him to me so many years ago. He told me that it was my smile that draws everyone to me, and that it gives people comfort and hope. My smile and recipes, he assured me, are bringing back to others memories of their childhood, their heritage, and their departed loved ones, who filled their bellies and their hearts.

Some people say traditions are not to be changed. Some say, "Out with the old, and in with the new." I say you have to find a happy medium. Allow those who want to turn away from tradition to make some changes; it just might bring them back to you. For those who are just starting out, remember that it is okay to borrow from the past; it is how you keep memories alive, and make new ones at the same time.

In short, it is important to remember the past and embrace the future. I believe that a classic recipe for happiness always has the wisdom and experience of something old blended with the dreams and youth of something new. Enjoy and pass the spoon to the younger generation; they hold the future. So until the next chapter, I wish you joy and happiness around your table.

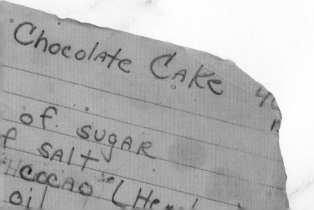

As a delivery boy years ago, Luigi would deliver meat from the butcher to Elisa. Now, 60 years later, Elisa still shops in what is now Luigi's store.

Acknowledgments

It is important in life to acknowledge the people who encourage you and support you unconditionally and professionally. I would like to give my continued thanks to my family, who allow me to have those moments, then embrace me until the pain goes away. To the residents of Divine Providence Village, who give me purpose every day, and have seen me through the good and the bad. And to my friends, who are always one step behind me when I need their shoulders to lean on.

For those who helped build this amazing collection of recipes, stories, and photographs, I want to especially thank David and Gabriella Versano, Lisa Jane Russell, Bryan Bechtel, and John and Luigi of Luigi and Giovanni's in Newtown Square, for their dedication and commitment to me and this project. Thank you to my literary agent, Judy Linden, and the team at Sterling Publishing. *Chiedo a Dio di benedirvi con grande fortuna nella vostra vita.*

Metric Chart

Liquid Measures

½ qt = ½ pt = 1 cup = 8 fl oz

¼ gal = 1 qt = 2 pt = 4 cups = 32 fl oz

½ gal = 2 qt = 4 pt = 8 cups = 64 fl oz

1 gal = 4 qt = 8 pt = 16 cups = =128 fl oz

Dry Measures

1 cup = 16 Tbsp = 48 tsp = 250 ml

¾ cup = 12 Tbsp = 36 tsp = 175ml

⅔ cup = 10 ⅔ Tbsp = 32 tsp = 150ml

½ cup = 8 Tbsp = =24 tsp = 125ml

⅓ cup = 5 ⅓ Tbsp = 16 tsp = 75 ml

¼ cup = 4 Tbsp = 12 tsp = 50ml

⅛ cup = 2 Tbsp = 6 tsp = 30ml

1 Tbsp = 3 tsp = 15 ml

Dash or Pinch or Speck=less than ⅛ tsp

Quickies

1 fl oz = 30 ml

1 oz = 28.35 g

1 lb = 16 oz (454 g)

1 kg = 2.2 lb

1 quart = 2 pints

U.S.	Metric
¼ tsp	1.25 mL
½ tsp	2.5 ml
1 tsp	5 ml
1 tb	15 ml
¼ cup	50 ml
⅓ cup	75 ml
½ cup	125 ml
⅔ cup	150 ml
¾ cup	175 ml
1 cup	250 ml
1 quart	1 liter

Recipe Abbreviations

Cup = c or C

Fluid = fl

Gallon = gal

Ounce = oz

Package = pkg

Pint = pt

Pound = lb or #

Quart = qt

Square = sq

Tablespoon = T or Tbl or TBSP or TBS

Teaspoon = t or tsp

Fahrenheit (ºF) to Celcius (ºC) $ºC = (F-32) \times 5/9$

ºF	ºC
32ºF	0ºC
40ºF	4ºC
140ºF	60ºC
150ºF	65ºC
160ºF	70ºC
225ºF	107ºC
250ºF	135ºC
275ºF	135ºC
300ºF	150ºC
325ºF	165ºC
350ºF	177ºC
375ºF	190ºC
400ºF	205ºC
425ºF	220ºC
450ºF	230ºC
475ºF	245ºC
500ºF	260ºC

Oven Temperatures

Warming: 200ºF

Very Slow: 250ºF-275ºF

Slow: 300ºF-375ºF

Moderate: 350ºF-375ºF

Hot: 400ºF-425ºF

Very Hot: 450º-475ºF

*Some measurements were rounded

Index